AN ILLUSTRATED GUIDE TO

MUSHROOMS

AND OTHER FUNGI

OF BRITAIN AND NORTHERN EUROPE

GEOFFREY KIBBY

First Published in 1992

This edition published in 1997 by

Parkgate Books Ltd
London House
Great Eastern Wharf
Parkgate Road
London SW11 4NQ
Great Britain

1 3 5 7 9 8 6 4 2

A catalogue record for this book is available from the British Library.

ISBN 1 85585 356 6

Printed and bound in Italy

AN ILLUSTRATED GUIDE TO

MUSHROOMS

AND OTHER FUNGI

OF BRITAIN AND NORTHERN EUROPE

GEOFFREY KIBBY

PARKGATE
BOOKS

CONTENTS

INTRODUCTION

FUNGI: THE UNKNOWN KINGDOM

For most people mushrooms and other fungi are very much an unknown world. Even though they may be very familiar with the flowers, birds or animals in their area, the fungi are often hardly noticed. Indeed many of us can probably remember as children being warned not to touch the 'poisonous toadstools', and have carried this image for years afterwards. This is a great pity since although there are some poisonous and even deadly species, the vast majority are harmless, some are delicious edibles and many are strikingly beautiful. All are fascinating in their manner of growth and dispersal and some are among the most remarkable organisms in the world in both appearance and life history.

Anyone just beginning to explore this unknown kingdom will soon realize that it is a vast and unending search that can easily enthrall you throughout your life. In Britain and northern Europe alone there are at least 2,000 larger fungi. These are just species which can easily be seen with the naked eye and do not include the thousands of other species best examined with the aid of a lens or microscope. If you extend your search to the other areas of the world – the Americas, Asia, Africa – the numbers rapidly climb to many thousands of species, many as yet unknown and undescribed. There is almost no part of the world in which some fungi cannot be found, from humid jungles to dry deserts, from arctic mountain tops to your own back garden, and it is this enormous variety of habitats that adds to the pleasure of studying fungi.

This book hopes to introduce you to some of the variety and beauty of mushrooms to be found in Britain and mainland northern Europe. Naturally, with so many species available to choose from I cannot hope to show you them all. What I have illustrated and described here are over 450 of the most spectacular, most important or otherwise easily identifiable species you are likely to find. Also included are a number of rare or little-known species, since you are certain to come across at least a few of the less common species and it adds a certain enjoyment to anticipate finding a rarity.

Wherever possible the edibility of each species is indicated. This is of ever-increasing interest as it is realized that mushrooms can add a very different flavour and texture to a dish. For a great many this data is either unknown, or the mushroom is too small or tough to eat. These species are usually classed as simply inedible. *It cannot be stressed enough that you must not take chances with eating fungi.* Only those which you have had accurately identified should be eaten; the risks of anything less are just too high and may be deadly. Individual reactions to any foods, even those usually regarded as edible, also vary and some people find certain species upset their stomachs when others find them edible and delicious. Always try just a small sample of any new edible at first to see whether you have any adverse reactions. The author and publishers cannot assume responsibility for the consequences of readers eating wild mushrooms. **Deadly species are indicated with a red skull and crossbones, species that are toxic but not normally deadly with a blue skull and crossbones.**

MUSHROOMS AND TOADSTOOLS - WHAT IS THE DIFFERENCE?

When people in Britain hear the word mushroom they usually think of the white variety they buy in their local supermarket, or perhaps the white field mushrooms they may have collected in the countryside when they were young. Almost everything else is classed as a toadstool. However, if you ask someone in Europe or North America what names they use, the answers would be very different. In parts of Europe dozens of different fungi are eaten and are commonly on sale in markets, and each variety may have its own name. Inedible or poisonous species may also have their own names. The split into two groups so prevalent in Britain is rarely made elsewhere. This reflects the very different historical attitudes to fungi of the different peoples and countries of the world. Britain and one or two other countries are often referred to as mycophobes (fungi-haters), while other countries such as France, Italy and Sweden are definitely mycophiles (fungi-lovers). The British have rarely eaten more than two or three species of fungi and have always looked with suspicion at the remainder. Europeans (and now many Americans) have always included fungi as a major part of their diet and are much more practised at identifying edible and poisonous species.

The words mushroom and toadstool have no scientific meaning and give no accurate guide to edibility or otherwise. They are simply cultural terms used historically (and very vaguely) by different people in different ways. In this book all species are simply referred to as either mushrooms or fungi regardless of edibility.

WHAT IS A FUNGUS?

The mushroom we see in the woods and fields is only a small part of the entire organism, just the part we can actually see. Usually hidden from sight are masses of almost invisible fungal threads called hyphae (the mycelium), which form the active feeding and growing structures of the fungus. The mushroom we see is solely for the production of the spores by which the fungus reproduces itself. This is analogous to the apple on a tree, with the tree representing the mycelium and the apple the mushroom fruiting body. Because of this it is possible to collect the fruiting body without damaging the total fungus. As long as the habitat is not disturbed and reasonable discretion shown in the number of specimens collected, the fungus will carry on growing and fruiting quite happily.

Most biologists now place the fungi entirely separate from, but related to, the other two major kingdoms with which we are familiar – plants and animals. Although in the distant past they probably shared an ancestry with primitive amoeba-like or algae-like organisms, they have since diverged in their own unique way. Unlike the green plants, they do not contain the pigment chlorophyll, so they cannot produce their own food through the action of sunlight. Instead they must feed directly on other organisms, either living or dead. Many fungi feed on dead and decaying vegetation or wood, or even dead animals, while others have evolved to become active parasites and attack living plants and animals, including human beings. Most people have heard of or been 'attacked' by athlete's foot, a common and very persistent fungal infection.

Thankfully the larger fungi usually confine their parasitic attacks to trees and other plants. Many fungi, however, have developed a fascinating and remarkable association with plants which is called mycorrhiza, whereby the mycelium of the fungi surround and penetrate the roots of the plant and they begin to swap nutrients back and forth. The association is extremely complex and benefits both fungus and plant; indeed, many forest trees are apparently unable to grow successfully without their fungal partners. Because of this association it is possible to predict in many cases which fungi will be growing with which tree. Some fungi may grow with a number of tree partners while others, such as *Suillus grevillei,* grow only under one type.

All the larger fungi will produce their spores in one of two basic ways. The majority of the species in this book form their spores externally on a club-like cell called a basidium, and are therefore placed in the class Basidiomycetes. The remainder produce their spores inside a long cell called an ascus and form the class Ascomycetes. These two major groups are further subdivided. In the case of the Basidiomycetes there are different types of basidium. Those with a simple, undivided basidium form the subclass Holobasidiomycetes, while those with basidia divided either longitudinally or laterally form the subclass

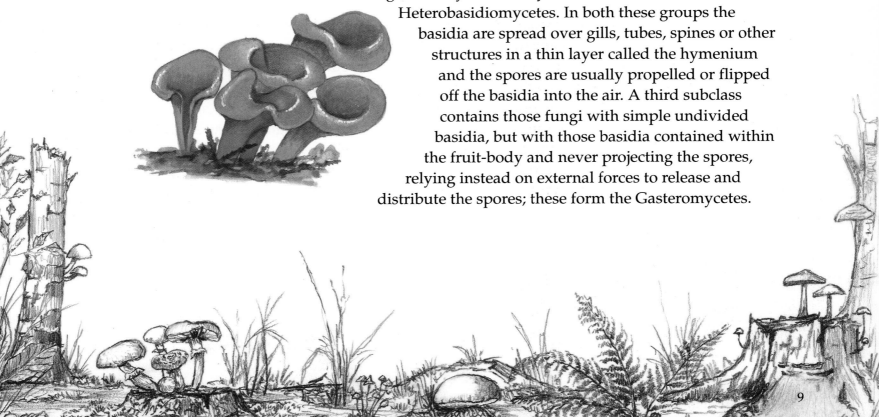

Heterobasidiomycetes. In both these groups the basidia are spread over gills, tubes, spines or other structures in a thin layer called the hymenium and the spores are usually propelled or flipped off the basidia into the air. A third subclass contains those fungi with simple undivided basidia, but with those basidia contained within the fruit-body and never projecting the spores, relying instead on external forces to release and distribute the spores; these form the Gasteromycetes.

These subclasses are further broken down into orders and then into families based on both visible and microscopic characters, chemical reactions, methods of spore dispersal and many other features. Nine principal orders of Basidiomycetes are dealt with here. These are once again subdivided, this time into genera, then finally into species. In the class Ascomycetes there are a great many orders, mostly outside the scope of this book, so only four are dealt with here: the Pezizales, Tuberales, Helotiales and Xylariales. Once again it is the details of microscopic characteristics that play a great part in determining these divisions.

HOW TO COLLECT AND STUDY FUNGI

With such an enormous number of species available, and those species varying somewhat with age and locality, it may seem a difficult job to identify them with any certainty. For some groups this is quite true and they are best dealt with by advanced amateurs and professionals using specialist literature. Examples of such groups include the genera *Psathyrella*, *Coprinus*, *Inocybe* and *Cortinarius.* However, many fungi are very distinctive and with careful collecting, some detailed observation and practice you will soon find yourself recognizing a number of the commoner species.

To increase your chances of making a correct identification some basic procedures should be followed. First, the material must be collected correctly. You want to minimize any damage to the specimen and make sure that you get the entire mushroom. So, for example, with a typical gilled mushroom with a cap and stem you should carefully lift the specimen out of the soil using a knife or trowel, making sure you do not leave any part of the stem behind. In many mushrooms, such as species of *Amanita,* this is vital since there may be a volval sac at the stem base. Try to avoid handling the specimen as many species have delicate features which bruise easily and rub off or even change colour when touched. It should then be carefully wrapped in a piece of waxed paper with the ends twisted like a sweet wrapper. This helps to stop the specimens being crushed in a bag or basket and also keeps moisture in the specimen. **Never use plastic bags.** Fungi soon sweat and collapse and stick to the sides forming a mush which is impossible to identify. When you get the specimens home, make careful notes on colour, texture, any rings or bags on the stem, smell the gills and even taste a tiny portion. The latter may seem alarming to the beginner but if only a tiny portion is rolled on the tongue and then spat out, it is quite safe, even with poisonous species. However, most mycologists make a point of learning well-known poisonous species to avoid having to taste them. Taste is very important in many groups, varying from mild to peppery or burning, bitter, or otherwise distinctive.

The next important step is make a spore print or deposit since it is vital to know the colour of the spores (this is not usually done in the case of Gasteromycetes). This is very easy and great fun to do since the colours vary from pure white to rust brown, pink, purple or even black. Simply place a mushroom cap with the gills, tubes or other spore-bearing surface down on a sheet of white paper and cover with a container for a few hours. After this period carefully lift the mushroom cap, and underneath you should have a good deposit of spores (it is often possible to peek under much sooner and so determine the colour that is forming). Let the deposit dry for a few minutes, then scrape them carefully together to determine the colour as accurately as possible.

The size of the spores is very important, as is their shape and whether they have any warts or spines. For this a microscope is required, although it is possible to study mushrooms without one. A microscope is nevertheless a great asset and often vital for the identification of many species as well as being a very enjoyable and fascinating hobby. The spores of all species are described and the microscopic details of length and breadth given. For example, spores 7–8 x 4–5μm means that the spores vary from 7 to 8 micrometres in length and 4 to 5 micrometres in width. A micrometre (often called a micron) is one thousandth of a millimetre.

Some basic chemical reactions are given and some of these chemicals are easily obtainable, for example, ammonia (window cleaner with ammonia will do) or caustic soda, KOH. Others are more specialized and their formulae given in the glossary.

Few mushrooms have a common name, only the well-known edible or poisonous species, most are called by their scientific name. This should not cause problems; after all, we speak of chrysanthemums and pelargoniums, and these are scientific names. The mushroom's scientific name consists of two Latinized words followed by the names of the authors who described the mushroom. For example, if we look at *Russula lutea* (Hudson ex Fries) S.F. Gray, the first name is the genus (*Russula*) always with a capital letter and in italics, while the second name is the specific epithet (*lutea*), always in lower case italics. It was described by Fries based on the earlier description of Hudson, but moved to the genus *Russula* by S.F. Gray. As many mushrooms have been placed in different genera by different authors and as the names may vary from guide book to guide book, the most well-known synonyms are given wherever possible. Remember, the mushrooms do not change, just our ideas about them.

PICTORIAL KEY TO MAJOR GROUPS

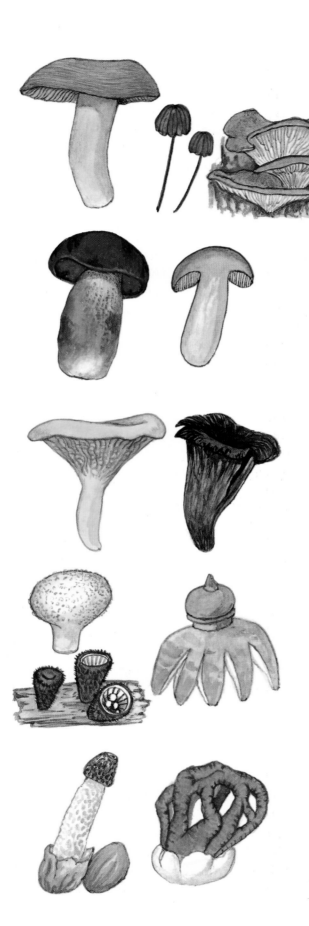

Mushrooms with gills:
These form the largest portion of the book. They include species both with and without stems, and are found both on the ground and on trees. They vary from the most delicate, fragile forms to large, robust fruiting bodies. All have radial flaps of tissue called gills, or lamellae. The thickness, attachment to the stem and the spacing of these gills can be important characteristics for separating different genera and species – see pages 37–134.

Boletes:
Fleshy fungi with a cap and stem similar to some gilled mushrooms, but rather than gills on the underside of the cap they have a layer of vertical, spongy tubes with the openings forming a layer of pores. The size and arrangement of these pores varies from genus to genus – see pages 18–36.

Chanterelles:
Sometimes confused with the gilled mushrooms and vice versa, but they never have true, narrow gills. Instead they have blunt-edged wrinkles, often multiply-forked and intervened with cross-ridges. Some forms are almost completely smooth on the outer surface of their trumpet-like forms – see pages 135–7.

Puffballs, Earthstars and Birds Nests:
Never with gills or pores, they all have some form of ball-like structure containing the spores, often elevated on a stalk or, as in the Earthstars, with an outer skin which splits into star-like arms. In the Birds Nests these spore masses are very tiny and contained in a cup- or nest-like structure – see pages 157–65.

Stinkhorns:
Bizarre fungi that 'hatch' from an egg, and whose spores are spread over specialized structures. The spores liquefy to produce a foul odour, hence the common name, and are usually eaten, and so dispersed, by insects – see pages 154–6.

Toothed Fungi:

Fungi with a cap and stem, and hence growing on the ground; or completely stemless and shelf-like; or even like undersea corals growing on a tree. All share the common feature of downward-pointing spines, or teeth, on which the spores are formed. The spines vary from extremely tiny and densely packed to over an inch in length and more widely spaced – see pages 144–6.

Polypores, Bracket Fungi and Crust Fungi:

Often very hard, or at least very tough and fleshy fungi, usually with one or more layers of downward-pointing tubes on the undersurface. The majority grow on trees, although some are found on soil. The crust-like fungi may or may not have a tube layer. Some polypores and brackets can grow from year to year, others are annuals and produce a new body each year – see pages 143–53.

Club and Coral Fungi:

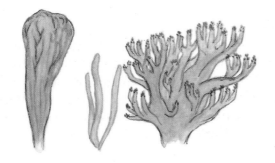

These fungi range from the simplest of club-shaped fruiting bodies to extremely complex and quite large coral-like structures where the clubs are multiply-branched, and forked at the tips. The majority grow on the ground, although there are exceptions. The spores are produced over most of the outer surface of the clubs – see pages 138–42, 176–6 and 178–9.

Jelly Fungi:

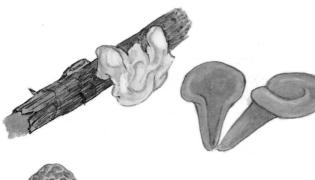

Very variable in form and size, from almost microscopic blobs of shapeless jelly, to more complex shapes like ears or tongues, but all with a soft jelly-like or sometimes rubbery texture. They grow on both the ground and on trees. Their spore-forming basidia are divided internally by cross-walls, either longitudinally or transversely – see pages 166–8.

Morels, False Morels and Cup Fungi:

From the simplest of cups, often microscopic in size, to complex brain-like or sponge-like structures raised on a stem. They are usually brittle in texture. All form their spores in an ascus, the latter usually spread over the cup surface, or in the pits of the sponge-like forms. The spores may often be seen ejecting in a dust-like puff when the fungus is disturbed – see pages 170–7.

DEVELOPMENT OF A MUSHROOM WITH VOLVA AND RING

The universal veil (1) enclosing the mushroom ruptures to leave a volva (4) at the base and fragments on the cap. The partial veil (3) covers the gills (2) and then is pulled away to form a ring on the stem. This is the most advanced form of veil development, other mushrooms may just have the partial veil (3), the universal veil (4) or, of course, no veils at all.

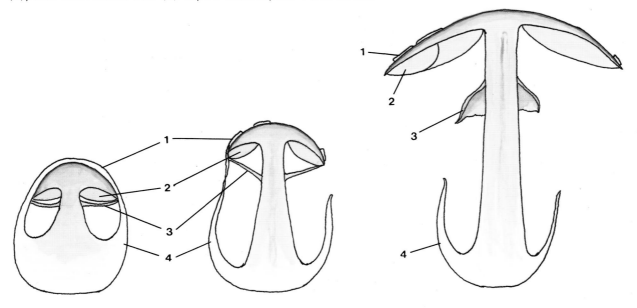

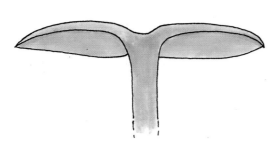

TYPES OF GILLS ATTACHMENT TO THE STEM AND CAP SHAPES

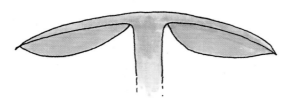

Free gills are completely clear of the stem, they are shown here on a rounded or convex cap.

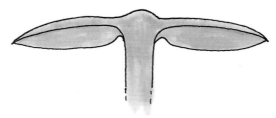

Sinuate or notched gills have a sudden curve just before they join the stem, often with a slight downward bend where they touch. The cap has a central bump or dome and is called umbonate.

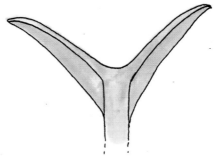

Adnate gills join the stem over their entire width (if they do not join on part of their width they are often described as adnexed), this cap has a central hollow and is described as depressed, if the depression is extreme, like a navel, then it is called umbilicate.

Decurrent gills join the stem and run down it for a greater or lesser amount, in some mushrooms it can be quite extreme; this cap is funnel shaped or infundibuliform.

COMMON MUSHROOM STRUCTURES

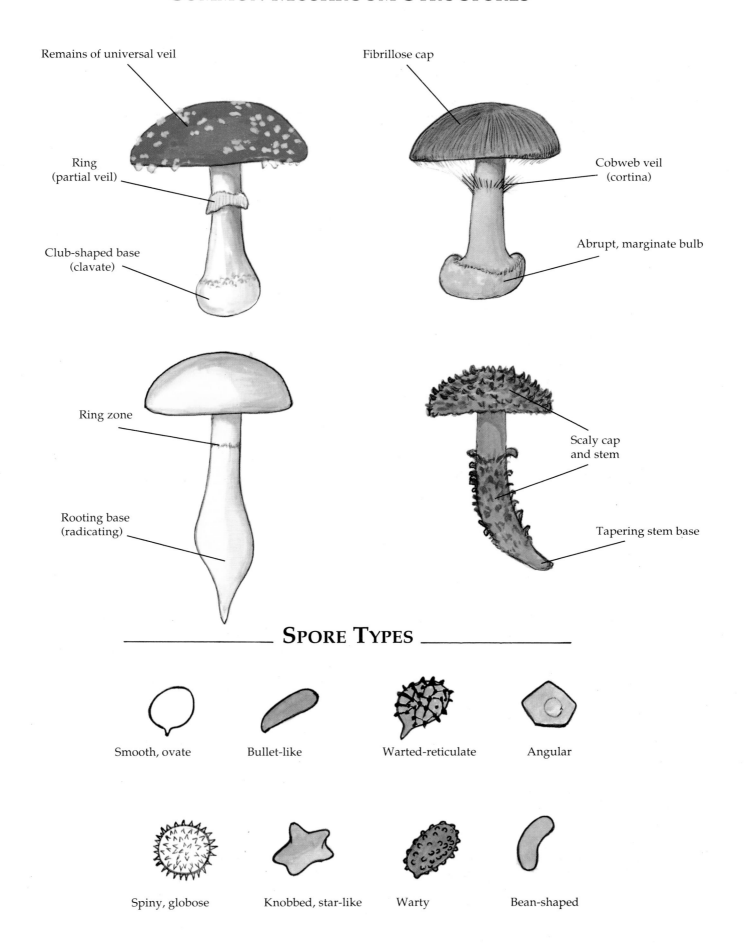

Remains of universal veil

Ring
(partial veil)

Club-shaped base
(clavate)

Fibrillose cap

Cobweb veil
(cortina)

Abrupt, marginate bulb

Ring zone

Rooting base
(radicating)

Scaly cap
and stem

Tapering stem base

SPORE TYPES

Smooth, ovate

Bullet-like

Warted-reticulate

Angular

Spiny, globose

Knobbed, star-like

Warty

Bean-shaped

EXAMPLES OF DIFFERENT BASIDIA

Holobasidiomycetes
(Typical Mushroom)

The basidia here are simple undivided cells, usually forming 1–4 spores on short sterigmata and arranged in a layer called the hymenium, spread over gills, tubes or other structures.

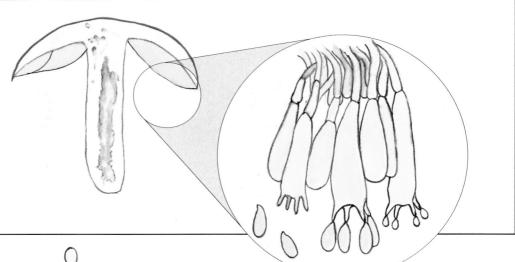

Heterobasidiomycetes
(Jelly Fungi)

Often rather strange, complex cells, with dividing cross-walls (septate) runnng either laterally or longitudinally. Usually 2-4 spores on extremely long sterigmata. Basidia are spread over the external surface of the fungus.

Auricularia species

Tremella species

Ascomycetes
(Cup Fungi)

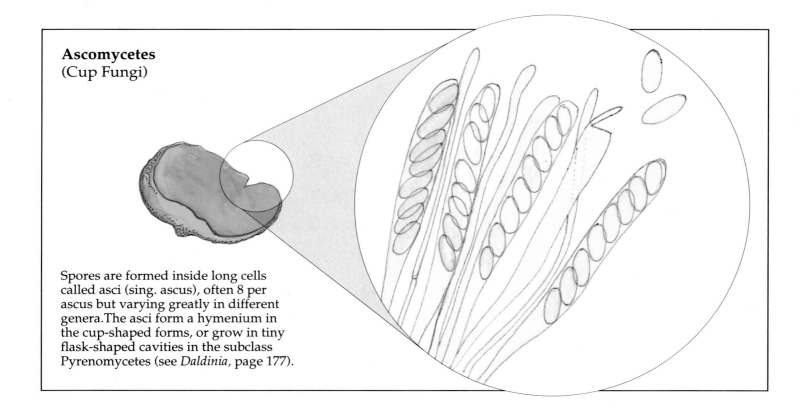

Spores are formed inside long cells called asci (sing. ascus), often 8 per ascus but varying greatly in different genera. The asci form a hymenium in the cup-shaped forms, or grow in tiny flask-shaped cavities in the subclass Pyrenomycetes (see *Daldinia*, page 177).

CLASS BASIDIOMYCETES

This class of fungi includes the majority of those illustrated in this book. They all share the common feature of producing their spores externally on a club-shaped or complex cell called a basidium, usually forming either two or four spores, although other numbers can be found. These basidia may form in an external layer called the hymenium or may form in a mass called the gleba, within the fruiting body. The Basidiomycetes are further divided into three subclasses based on the structure of the basidium, the Holobasidiomycetes, Heterobasidiomycetes and Gasteromycetes.

ORDER: BOLETALES

All boletes share common features: a soft, fleshy body; the basidia produced in a vertically arranged layer of minute tubes (the pores) on the underside of the cap; the forming of an association with specific trees. Their spores vary from round to – more commonly – long and bullet shaped. The spores may be smooth or ornamented and range in colour from yellowish to olive-brown, pinkish or even black.

Many species display a remarkable change in colour when their flesh is cut or bruised. This is caused by the reaction of certain chemicals in the flesh with oxygen and may be almost instantaneous. Some boletes have distinctive tastes or odours, and in others identification is often aided by the use of chemical tests.

In size they range from under 2cm (1in) to over 60cm (2ft) across the cap in some tropical species; even in Britain they can reach 30cm (12in). The Boletales also include some gilled mushrooms, namely *Paxillus, Phylloporus* and *Gomphidius,* but they are treated with the other gilled mushrooms for convenience since most beginners would expect to find them there.

BOLETACEAE
Bolete Family

These fungi include some of the most sought-after edible species. Mushrooms such as *Boletus edulis* are eaten all over the world either fresh, or dried in mushroom soups. Britain is rich in bolete species and they form one of the most attractive and readily visible groups of fungi throughout our woodlands.

Boletus edulis Bulliard ex Fries – 'Cep', 'Steinpilz' or 'Pennybun'
Cap: 10–25cm (4–10in)
Spores: 13–19 x 4–6.5μm
Edibility: edible and delicious

The most sought-after edible bolete in the world, it occurs over the whole northern temperate region of North America, Europe and Asia. It grows in both mixed conifer and deciduous woodlands and a number of varieties and subspecies have been described from under different trees. Distinguishing features are the young pores which are white, maturing to yellow-olive; the unchanging flesh when cut and the fine white network which covers the stem. The cap colour varies from a light yellow-brown to a deep reddish-brown, often with a lighter, whitish margin. The flesh has a mild, nutty flavour and dries well, making it invaluable in commercial mushroom soups. It is collected in enormous numbers in Europe for sale and processing, as well as for personal use.

Boletus aereus Bulliard ex Fries
Cap: 7.5–20cm (3–8in)
Spores: olive-brown,12–14 x 4–5μm
Edibility: edible and delicious

A wonderful species with its dark chocolate-brown to blackish cap, its often huge size and excellent flavour. The cap is dry and finely granular in texture, frequently cracking into a fine mosaic. When covered in leaves it becomes blotched with paler, discoloured patches. The tubes and pores are white to begin with but soon age to a yellowish colour. The stem is distinctive with a brownish ground overlaid with a darker, fine network overall, unlike the better known *B. edulis,* which has a pale, whitish stem. The flesh is white with a sweet, nutty flavour, making it a popular edible. Found under oaks, especially in the south of England, in late summer and through the autumn.

Boletus aestivalis Poulet ex Fries
Cap: 7.5–20cm (3–8in)
Spores: olive-brown, 14–17 x 4.5–5.5μm
Edibility: edible and excellent

This species usually grows earlier in the season – from late June onwards – than most of its relatives and can be very erratic in its fruitings. I have seen a hillside in Scotland covered with several hundred specimens one year but none the next. It differs from the more well-known *B. edulis* by its paler buff-brown to ochre cap which is dry and finely cracked when mature. The stem is also buff coloured with a fine white mesh overall. Most commonly found in the south, although widespread; it grows under beech and oak and is highly regarded as a good, edible species.

Boletus pinophilus Pilat & Dermek
Cap: 7.5–20cm (3–8in)
Spores: olive-brown, 14–17 x 4.5–5.5μm
Edibility: edible and good

A close relative of the well-known Cep Bolete, *Boletus edulis,* this species differs in its redder, or more purplish-brown cap colours and reddish-brown stem with fine white network overall. The flesh is firm and white with a reddish flush under the cap skin. The pores are white at first then soon yellowish. Quite common under pines in Scotland and parts of England; this is a particularly attractive species.

Boletus impolitus Fries
Cap: 5–15cm (2–6in)
Spores: olive-brown, 9–16 x 4–6μm
Edibility: edible but of poor quality

One of the few boletes to be distinguished by its smell, there is often a strong odour of iodine or of old-fashioned school ink, especially in the stem base. The yellowish-ochre to buff-grey cap is finely velvet to matt. The tubes and pores are rather bright yellow but do not change colour when bruised. The stem is swollen with a pale yellowish surface finely dotted with minute woolly flecks; the base is often slightly rooting and tapered. The flesh is firm and white or flushed slightly reddish. A rather uncommon species, usually under oaks.

Boletus regius Krombholtz
Cap: 7.5–20cm (3–8in)
Spores: olive-brown, 12–16.5 x 3.5–5μm
Edibility: edible but often spoiled by insects

It is unfortunate that this is such a rare species in Britain as it is one of our most beautiful boletes. The cap varies from rose-red to dark-red and is smooth to slightly fibrous. The tubes and pores are bright yellow bruising blue when handled. The robust stem is bright-yellow flushed pink and has a fine network overall. The flesh is yellowish and stains pale blue, sometimes not at all. Very uncommon to rare, it is found in southern England, usually under oaks or beeches. A second species – *B. speciosus* – is distinguished by some authors by its duller, reddish-brown to blood-red cap, and flesh staining dark blue when cut.

Boletus appendiculatus Schaeffer ex Fries

Cap: 10–20cm (4–8in)

Spores: olive-brown, 12–15 x 3.5–5µm

Edibility: edible and quite good when young

The dry, slightly fibrous cap is a rich brick-red to cinnamon-brown. The tubes and pores are bright yellow and bruise deep blue when touched. The stem is also yellow, with a fine, concolorous network over the upper half, often flushed reddish-brown at the base. The flesh is yellow, flushing pale blue when cut, and can have a rather strong, rank odour when mature. It grows under oak and beech, often in large numbers, and especially so in southern England.

Boletus calopus Fries

Cap: 7.5–20cm (3–8in)

Spores: olive-brown, 10–14 x 4–6µm

Edibility: inedible, extremely bitter to taste

The bitter flavour of the flesh spoils what is otherwise a beautiful species. The rose-red to crimson stem has a fine white network overall while the cap is a dull ochre to pale, whitish-buff. The pores are yellow and bruise pale blue, as does the flesh. A widespread, though seldom common species under beech or pine.

Boletus albidus Rocques

Cap 7.5–20cm (3–8in)

Spores: olive-brown, 12–16 x 4.5–6µm

Edibility: inedible, very bitter although not poisonous

This species can present the appearance of a large worn stone from the top and might even be passed over by the inexperienced collector. At first dingy white the cap soon becomes dirty buff to olive-grey, with a slightly velvety then smooth surface. The tubes and pores are bright lemon-yellow, bruising blue. The stem is usually fat and swollen, often rooting, a pale lemon-yellow with a very fine network of the same colour, which is often reduced or even absent. The flesh is whitish-yellow, turning very pale blue when cut and has an extremely bitter taste. Rather uncommon, this beautiful species is found under beech and oak in southern and central Britain.

Boletus erythropus Persoon

Cap: 5–15cm (2–6in)

Spores: 11–19 x 4.5–7µm

Edibility: apparently edible but best avoided like all blue-staining species

The cap colour varies from rich, chocolate-brown to pale yellowish-brown and the surface can be almost velvety when young although it will soon become smooth with age. The pores are usually deep, almost blood-red but may be paler, more orange, in colder weather. The stem is yellowish-orange overlaid with very fine red dots (you may need to use a hand-lens), presenting a generally red appearance. The flesh is yellow but instantly flushes deep blue when cut. Common throughout Britain in mixed woods, especially oak and beech.

Boletus pseudosulphureus Kallenbach

Cap: 7.5–10cm (3–4in)

Spores:10–16 x 5–6.5µm

Edibility: inedible

An exceptionally attractive species with its bright yellow cap, it becomes browner with age and all parts bruise deep blue when handled. The tubes and pores are yellow sometimes flushed slightly orange. The stem is yellow with slightly darker, fine woolly dots. The flesh is bright yellow rapidly turning deep blue when cut. This very rare mushroom must be considered a prize find in Britain where it is found under beech and oak.

Boletus luridus Schaeffer ex Fries

Cap: 7.5–12.5cm (3–5in)

Spores: 9–17 x 5–7µm

Edibility: doubtful; has been reported to cause poisoning

This is perhaps the commonest of a group of species which all have red pores, a prominent network on the stem and flesh which turns blue when cut. In this species the matt cap varies from pale orange-ochre to yellow-buff, becoming more olive with age. The tubes are yellow while the pore mouths are orange-red and bruise deep blue. The cylindrical stem is yellowish with a prominent red network overall. The flesh is yellowish, often deep purple-red in the stem base, and instantly turns blue when cut. This species is not uncommon under beech and oak on calcareous soils, particularly in the south.

Boletus queletii Schultzer

Cap: 7.5–12.5cm (3–5in)

Spores: 10–17 x 5–8µm

Edibility: uncertain, best avoided

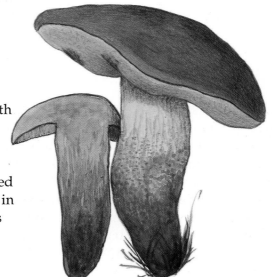

Sadly a rather rare species, but certainly one of our most striking with a rich brick to orange-red cap with a velvety surface when young, becoming smooth with age. The tubes are yellow with the pores a striking shade of apricot-orange. The pores bruise deep blue when touched. The stem is yellowish with tiny red dots and is often pointed and rooting at the base. The flesh is yellow flushed deep purple-red in the base, and turns blue when cut. It seems to prefer calcareous soils under beech, oak and lime in southern England.

Boletus satanus Lenz – 'Satan's Bolete'

Cap: 7.5–30cm (3–12in)

Spores: 11–15 x 4–6µm

Edibility: poisonous; causes acute gastric distress

The mycologist who described this species stated that its emanations were so malign that he felt ill even at a distance. Although no one else has reported these effects to quite this extent, the present author once had to remove a specimen from the room because of the awful stench that it emitted. This often huge, bulky bolete has a white cap when young, soon becoming a pallid grey-white to olive-white with age. The swollen, obese stem has a fine, red network over a paler red background. The blood-red minute pores bruise blue as does the pale yellow flesh. The odour soon becomes strong and nauseous, like rotting garlic, and the mushroom is one of the very few boletes to cause poisoning when eaten. An uncommon species found under beech and oak on calcareous soils in central and southern England.

Boletus splendidus Martin

Cap: 10–15cm (4–6in)

Spores: 11–13 x 4.5–6µm

Edibility: uncertain, possibly poisonous

Formerly confused with the previous species, it differs in its cap being greyish-white to almost olive but soon flushed with pink. The tubes are yellow with deep, blood-red pore mouths which bruise blue. The stem is robust, but not as obese as in *B. satanus*, and is dull yellow with a purplish-red network especially on the upper half. The flesh is lemon-yellow and flushes very pale blue when cut. The odour is slightly spicy but not nauseating as in *B. satanus*. A rare species, it occurs under beech and oak in southern and central England, usually on calcareous soils.

Boletus rhodopurpureus Smotlaka
Cap: 10–20cm (4–8in)
Spores: 14–18 x 5.5–6.5μm
Edibility: possibly poisonous

This species is almost chameleon-like in the range and variety of colour changes that it can undergo. The cap is at first grey-brown to pinkish-grey but soon becomes flushed purple-red overall as it matures. The tubes are yellow with blood-red pore openings which bruise blue. The stem is stout, swollen and yellowish, with a fine purple-red network overall. The flesh is bright yellow and turns bright blue when cut, and there is often a strong, fruity odour present. A very rare species found under beech and oak on calcareous soils in southern England, it is one of our most striking and distinctive boletes.

Boletus subtomentosus Linnaeus ex Fries
Cap: 5–10cm (2–4in)
Spores: 11–14 x 4–6μm
Edibility: edible but poor quality

The velvety cap is olive-yellow to rich yellow, becoming smoother and more reddish-brown with age or handling. The tubes and pores are bright yellow, large and angular, and do not turn blue when bruised. The stem is narrow and tapered, dull olive-yellow to cream-buff and often has some coarse ridges or furrows on the upper half. The flesh is white and almost unchanging. A drop of ammonia placed on the cap turns dull brown, **not** blue-green as in *B. lanatus.* This is a common species in deciduous woods throughout Britain.

Boletus lanatus Rostkovius
Cap: 2.5–10cm (1–4in)
Spores: 9–11.5 x 3.5–4.5μm
Edibility: edible, but poor quality

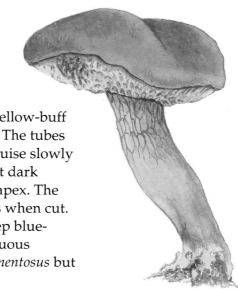

This can be a beautiful species with its velvety cap of deep yellow-buff or cinnamon, becoming darker brown with age or handling. The tubes and pores are bright yellow, rather large and angular, and bruise slowly blue on handling. The stem is yellowish-buff with prominent dark brick-coloured veins, often forming a coarse network at the apex. The flesh is white, pale yellow in the stem base, and hardly blues when cut. A drop of household ammonia placed on the cap turns a deep blue-green. This is a common species to be found in mixed deciduous woods throughout Britain. It is often confused with *B. subtomentosus* but is easily separated by the green ammonia reaction.

Boletus chrysenteron Fries

Cap: 5–8cm (2–3in)
Spores: 9–13 x 3.5–5μm
Edibility: edible, but of poor quality

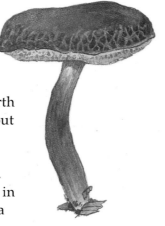

Perhaps the best known of the smaller boletes both in Europe and North America, this species is to be found in almost any woodland throughout Britain. The brownish cap soon develops fine cracks which expose the reddish flesh beneath. The pores are yellowish and bruise blue. The slender stem is yellowish-white above, shading to purplish-red below, and has pale flesh which also stains blue when cut. Although variable in cap colour (more olive or reddish forms are common), the cracking is a consistent feature of older specimens.

Boletus pruinatus Fries

Cap: 5–10cm (2–4in)
Spores: 11.5–14.5 x 4.5–5.5μm
Edibility: edible and quite good

At the season's end, when the weather becomes colder and the leaf litter is already deep on the forest floor, this species makes its appearance, and it is one of our most beautiful boletes. The cap is a deep purple-brown, chestnut or almost black at the centre with the margin usually red; it is covered in a hoary bloom like a grape. The tubes and pores are bright yellow, slowly turning blue when bruised. The stem is smooth and bright chrome-yellow with the base flushed slightly reddish. The flesh is also bright golden-yellow, staining slowly blue, which distinguishes it easily from the related *B. chrysenteron*. This is a characteristic species of our southern beech woods.

Boletus porosporus Imler

Cap: 5–7.5cm (2–3in)
Spores: 12–17 x 4–6.5μm one end of each spore is distinctly flattened or truncated
Edibility: edible but poor

A rather dull, almost ugly species at times, the matt or velvety cap is a dull, olive-brown and soon becomes cracked, exposing whitish flesh beneath. The tubes and pores are a dull olive-yellow, becoming even dingier with age, and may blue slightly when bruised. The stem is usually a dull greyish-olive to brown with a narrow reddish zone above and a brighter yellow above this zone. To observe the truncate spores a spore print must be taken. Spores taken from the tubes are rarely mature and are not yet flattened. This species was formerly confused with *B. chrysenteron* described above, before being distinguished by the dull colours and distinctive spores. A locally common species it is to be found under oaks and other deciduous trees throughout Britain.

Boletus leonis Reid

Cap: 2.5–7.5cm (1–3in)
Spores: 10–13 x 5–6µm
Edibility: edible

This is rather a rare species apparently confined to southern England, and has probably been confused with other species in the past. The surface of the cap is distinctly roughened to velvety and is a rich tawny-orange to yellow and often slightly cracked or scaly. The tubes and pores are bright yellow to olive-yellow and do not bruise blue. The stem is yellow-ochre and smooth to slightly woolly, and has firm, pale flesh. It seems to prefer grassy areas under oaks.

Boletus rubellus Krombholtz

Cap: 2–5cm (1–2in)
Spores: 7–17 x 4–7µm
Edibility: edible but poor

There are few boletes, or indeed any other fungi, as attractive as this small species. To see the clusters of bright scarlet or blood-red caps nestled deep in the grass along paths and woodland tracks where it likes to grow is of the delights of mushrooming. Both cap and stem are red and bruise blue when handled, while the pores are pale yellow. It is always found close to oak trees, usually out near the root tips in damp grass soon after the first of the late summer rains and is common throughout much of England. Although edible, insects find it attractive, so it is usually very 'wormy'.

Boletus rubinus W. G. Smith

Cap 2.5–5cm (1–2in)
Spores: 5.5–6.5 x 4–5µm
Edibility: edible but poor

A rare but very distinctive species with the most beautiful carmine-red pores; unlike most boletes they are decurrent down the short stem. Also unusual are the short, almost rounded spores. It might be mistaken for the related *Boletus piperatus* but that does not have decurrent pores and the taste is very peppery. The habitat differs also: *B. rubinus* grows exclusively under oaks in the south whereas *B. piperatus* occurs under birch or pine and is widespread throughout Britain.

Boletus piperatus Fries

Cap: 3–8cm (2–4in)

Spores: 9–12 x 4–5μm

Edibility: inedible, very peppery to taste

Unusual flavours are very rare in the majority of boletes, the most common being a bitter taste, but the hot, peppery flavour of this species is most distinctive. A small, pretty species, it has cinnamon to cinnabar-red pores and the stem is bright yellow at the base, as is the flesh inside. It occurs most commonly under birch and occasionally under pine and is widespread throughout Britain. It appears that there may be some sort of association with the Fly Agaric mushroom, *Amanita muscaria*, since the bolete has been observed on almost every occasion fruiting within a few inches of the *Amanita*.

Aureoboletus cramesinus (Secretan) Watling

Cap 2.5–7.5cm (1–3in)

Spores: 15–20 x 4–7μm

Edibility: edible but poor

This small species has perhaps the brightest golden-yellow pores of any British bolete. Under a microscope the tubes are seen to be lined with inflated cells called cystidia, each filled with bright yellow fluid which gives the tubes and pores their bright colour. Because of this and some other unusual features the bolete is placed in a new genus, *Aureoboletus.* The slightly sticky cap is a dull pinkish-brown and often irregularly streaked. The slender, tapered stem is yellow, flushed with reddish-brown, and is often sticky. The flesh is white, marbled with pinkish-brown. A rather uncommon species found under beech and oak on clay or calcareous soils in southern England.

Boletus parasiticus Fries

Cap 2.5–7.5cm (1–3in)

Spores: 12–18 x 3.5–5μm

Edibility: edible but not worthwhile

Quite unique and unmistakable among British boletes, this species has developed a most remarkable method of growth. It occurs only on fruit-bodies of the common Earthball, *Scleroderma citrinum*, often with several boletes pushing up from the base of the Earthball. It does not seem to cause undue damage to its host since the Earthball continues to produce its own spores, even though its tissues are invaded by the mycelium of the bolete. A locally common species, it may appear in large numbers in wet seasons.

Boletus pulverulentus Opatowski
Cap: 5–10cm (2–4in)
Spores: 11–14 x 4.5–6μm
Edibility: edible but not recommended

Although many fungi, and particularly boletes, change colour when cut or bruised, there are few mushrooms as remarkable as this species in the intensity of the change. When any part of the mushroom is handled, and particularly when cut open, there is an almost instantaneous change to the deepest cobalt blue or blue-black. When fresh the bolete has a reddish-brown cap with yellow pores and a yellow stem flushed with red. By the time you get it home it may be almost unrecognizable from the staining and bruising. This is a locally common species found mostly under oaks in the south and south-west.

Boletus badius Fries
Cap: 5–10cm (2–4in)
Spores: 10–14 x 4–5μm
Edibility: edible and good

Found throughout Britain and indeed across most of the temperate northern hemisphere, this chestnut-brown species has a slightly velvety cap when young, with yellowish-cream pores which bruise dull blue-grey. The cylindrical stem is smooth and coloured like the cap. It occurs in both conifer and deciduous woods, especially under beech. Specimens from the latter habitat tend to be brighter in colour and much more velvety and are sometimes referred to as a separate species, *B. vaccinus*, by some mycologists.

Boletus fragrans Vittadini
Cap: 7.5–12.5cm (3–5in)
Spores: 10–15 x 4.5–5.5μm
Edibility: edibility uncertain

This is an exceedingly rare species more often reported from southern Europe than in Britain, but may perhaps have been misidentified in the past. The cap is dark reddish-brown with a matt to greasy surface, while the tubes and pores are bright yellow. The stem is usually pointed and slightly rooting and is pale creamy-ochre, smooth, and darker reddish-brown to pinkish below. The flesh is white to pale yellow, sometimes turning faintly blue when cut. It may smell strongly of fruit or spice. The few records we have are from grassy areas under oaks and have been quite widespread.

Tylopilus felleus (Fries) Karsten

Cap: 5–20cm (2–8in)
Spores: 11–15 x 3–5μm
Edibility: inedible, extremely bitter to taste

Many a meal of mushrooms has been spoiled by this species, particularly when the collectors thought they were picking the delicious Cep Bolete – *Boletus edulis* – which this species resembles. However, one taste of this species will soon show you the error you have made. It tastes almost as bitter as quinine and the flavour is not improved by cooking. Like *Boletus edulis*, this species has a network on its stem, but unlike that species the overall coloration is yellow-brown and the mature pores take on a distinct pink flush. The spores differ also in their pinkish-brown to purplish colour. A common species under both pine and beech trees throughout Britain. Although there is only the one species in Great Britain, if you travel to North America, or to other parts of the world, there are numerous other, often very dramatically coloured and fascinating species. Many of them are equally bitter to taste.

Uloporus lividus (Fries) Quélet

Cap: 5–10cm (2–4in)
Spores: 4.5–6 x 3–4μm
Edibility: edible but rather poor

A rare and rather strange species, it is very restricted in its choice of habitat, growing only under species of alder, both European native species and also introduced species like the Japanese alder. It prefers deep, wet grassy tussocks around the base of trees and appears to be confined to woods south of the Scottish border. Unlike other boletes, the pores are deeply decurrent, lemon to greenish-yellow and often rather large and angular, bruising deep blue-grey. The smooth cap is quite sticky when wet, and a pale ochre-tan, as is the stem also. The spores are unusually short and rounded compared with those of most boletes, and paler and more yellowish in colour than the olive-brown of most species. It is frequently placed in another genus, *Gyrodon*, but this is a much disputed name amongst bolete specialists and I am here using the name given in the last British bolete monograph.

Leccinum carpini (Schulzer) Pearson

Cap: 5–10cm (2–4in)
Spores: 12–17 x 4.5–6μm
Edibility: edible

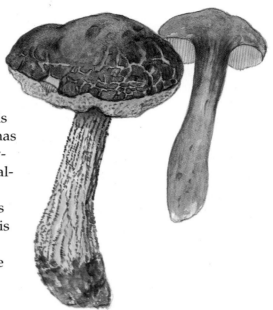

The genus *Leccinum* is distinguished by the woolly-squamulose stem, with the squamules usually starting pale and darkening with age. This species is one of the earliest to appear after the first summer rains. It has a strangely wrinkled, cracked cap and is a dark sepia-brown to tawny-brown, cracking as it ages. The pores are white to cream, bruising coral-pink then soon purplish-black. The stem is often long and slender, white with darker, sepia-brown, woolly scales. The white flesh bruises reddish-pink then soon purplish and finally black; in the stem base it is frequently bright blue. Found most commonly under hornbeam but also with hazel; widespread but especially in southern England where large stands of hornbeam are still to be found. To observe the colour changes in *Leccinum* cut the mushroom completely in half lengthwise and gently rub the surface of one half – then sit back and wait to see how it changes in comparison with the unrubbed half.

Leccinum holopus (Rostkovius) Watling

Cap: 5–10cm (2–4in)
Spores: 13–20 x 5–6μm
Edibility: edible but poor

White boletes are rather rare and distinctive, so they are usually easy to identify. This is the species you are most likely to come across in Britain, often in *Sphagnum* bogs, under birch and particularly in Scotland and northern England, although it can be found in the south. The whole mushroom is at first pure white but soon takes on a delicate blue-green to olive flush with age. The flesh in the stem base may often show a blue-green stain.

Leccinum duriusculum (Kalchbrenner & Schulzer) Singer

Cap: 7.5–12.5cm (3–5in)
Spores: 13–17 x 5–6μm
Edibility: edible and good

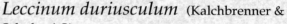

All *Leccinum* species are mycorrhizal, meaning that they grow in association with the roots of trees, and are usually very specific about which tree they pick. This species is no exception since it grows only with the common aspen, *Populus tremula*. A large, rather stout species, the dull grey-brown cap is often wrinkled or bumpy. The flesh is distinctive in its colour changes, flushing reddish-salmon then purplish-black to grey-black. It is not a common species, but if you have a stand of aspens nearby it is worth checking throughout the autumn.

Leccinum quercinum (Pilat) Green & Watling

Cap: 5–15cm (2–6in)
Spores: 12–15 x 3.5–5μm
Edibility: edible and excellent

The rich, fox-red to brick-red or even dark reddish-chestnut caps are strikingly beautiful set against the leaf litter of the oaks under which this species grows. The cap surface is minutely woolly-fibrous and may be slightly scaly at the centre, the cap cuticle overhangs the margin. The pores are cream to buff and bruise pinkish-brown. The stem is often stout, cream with dark foxy-brown woolly squamules. The flesh is white flushing pinkish-purple then soon purplish-grey, often greenish in the stem base. Quite common in some areas, especially in central and southern England.

Leccinum versipelle (Fries & Hök) Snell

Cap: 7.5–20cm (3–8in)
Spores: 12.5–16 x 4–5μm
Edibility: edible and excellent, widely collected

Often referred to as Red-caps by European collectors, this species is, in fact, shades of orange or yellow-tawny. The cap is minutely downy and often slightly scaly at the centre, the cap cuticle overhangs at the margin. The pores are cream bruising purplish-buff. The stout stem is white or greyish with dark, black-brown woolly squamules, the base of the stem is often flushed green. The flesh is white becoming livid purplish-pink then purplish-grey and finally blackish, often flushed green in the stem base. Very common and widespread wherever birches are found. When cooked the flesh may turn completely blackish but it still tastes very good.

Leccinum aurantiacum S. F. Gray

Cap: 5–15cm (2–6in)
Spores: 14–16.5 x 4–5μm
Edibility: edible and excellent

Once again this has a different host tree, in this instance under aspen, *Populus tremula*. The cap is a rich orange to brick-red with the cap cuticle overhanging the margin, and where covered by leaves often has pale, uncoloured patches. The pores are pale cream bruising pinkish-brown. The stem is cream with woolly squamules which start white at first but soon turn dark reddish-brown. The flesh is white turning reddish then purplish and finally greyish-brown. This species, plus *L. versipelle*, *L. duriusculum* and *L. quercinum*, form a closely related complex of species, but by observing their different cap colours combined with their different host trees they are usually easily distinguishable.

Leccinum crocipodium (Letellier) Watling
Cap: 5–10cm (2–4in)
Spores: 12–17.5 x 4.5–6μm
Edibility: edible and quite good

A totally yellow bolete is very distinctive, and when combined with the blackening flesh and a habitat under oaks recognition is quite easy. Starting a rich, deep yellow the cap soon turns a dull yellowish-brown to olive-brown. The surface is often irregular and lumpy and becomes minutely cracked and mosaic-like. The pores are bright yellow bruising brownish. The stem is stout, pale yellow with woolly squamules which become darker with age. The flesh is yellow then greyish-purple, chestnut and finally blackish. This species is often quite common under oaks in warm, wet years in southern England.

Leccinum variicolor Watling
Cap: 5–10cm (2–4in)
Spores: 12.5–16 x 4.5–6μm
Edibility: edible but poor

This can be one of our most striking species with its often oddly blotched and mottled cap. The latter is a drab, bluish-grey, grey-brown to almost blackish with white, discoloured areas. The pores are cream, bruising rose-pink. The stem is white with dark grey-brown to black woolly squamules on the lower half. The flesh is white turning bright rose-pink to reddish-salmon when cut (it is stronger when rubbed) and often bright blue-green in the base of the stem. Found under birch, this often very common species was formerly confused with *L. scabrum* which does not discolour when cut.

Leccinum scabrum (Fries) S. F. Gray
Cap: 5–15cm (2–6in)
Spores: 15–19 x 5–7μm
Edibility: edible and quite good

A common if rather nondescript species with a dull brown to buff cap, quite sticky in wet weather. The pores are whitish-buff, hardly changing when bruised. The slender stem is white to buff with small, darker brown woolly squamules. This is one of the few *Leccinum* species whose flesh hardly changes colour when cut, and it is also to be distinguished by the softness of the flesh in the cap; pressing the cap with your finger usually leaves a depression. There may, however, be bright blue-green stains at the base of the stem. Found under birch, it is widespread throughout Britain.

Leccinum roseofractum Watling

Cap: 5–10cm (2–4in)
Spores: 15–17 x 5.5–6µm
Edibility: edible and good

This species was formerly confused with *L. scabrum* from which it is distinguished by its robust stature, dark blackish-brown cap and woolly squamules, and flesh which stains a bright reddish-pink. There are never any blue-green stains at the base of the stem. The cap usually has a slightly greasy texture. The pores are cream bruising pinkish-purple then brown. Often quite common, it is found under birch throughout Britain. It may be confused with *L. variicolor* but the latter has a mottled grey-brown cap and blue-green stains in the stem.

Gyroporus castaneus (Fries) Quélet

Cap: 2.5–10cm (1–4in)
Spores: 8–12.5 x 5–6µm
Edibility: edible and delicious

The genus *Gyroporus* is distinguished by its ochre-yellow, broad spores and the brittle, firm stem which becomes hollow with irregular cavities. This attractive, rather small species is a rich cinnamon-brown to yellow-brown, with pale yellowish-cream pores. The flesh has a mild, nutty flavour. It is an uncommon species in Britain, usually occurring in the south, where it is found exclusively under oaks.

Gyroporus cyanescens (Fries) Quélet

Cap: 5–12.5cm (2–5in)
Spores: 8–10 x 5–6µm
Edibility: edible and quite good

This species cannot be mistaken for any other bolete with its overall whitish-straw colours combined with the quite remarkable depth of the colour change when cut. All parts turn an intense cobalt blue within a few moments of bruising or cutting. The stem is hollowed, as in other *Gyroporus* species, while the cap surface is fibrous and roughened. It is a rather uncommon species in Britain, being most plentiful in the north, where it is found under pines and birches on sandy soils.

Suillus granulatus (Fries) Kuntze
Cap 5–10cm (2–4in)
Spores: 7–10 x 2.5–3.5μm
Edibility: edible with caution, can cause stomach upsets

The genus *Suillus* is typified by the arrangement of special cells (cystidia) in the tubes, by the small, glandular dots on the upper part of the stem, by the often sticky cap (although a few species are dry and scaly) and by the strict relationship with particular species of conifer. This species has all of these features. The cap is cinnamon brown to orange-brown and the pores are pale yellow and often weep milky droplets when young. This is a common species under pine, often found in large numbers. Like many *Suillus* species, it may be eaten safely by some but cause stomach upsets in others.

Suillus luteus (Fries) S. F. Gray – 'Slippery Jack'
Cap: 5–10cm (2–4in)
Spores: 7–9 x 2.5–3μm
Edibility: edible with caution; can cause upsets

The common name refers to the viscid, glutinous cap in wet weather. The rich reddish-brown cap is often streaky or fibrous under the gluten. The stem is very distinctive with glandular dots at the apex and a thick, membranous white ring. The ring is usually flushed lilac on the underside. Although widely collected as a good edible, the viscid cap cuticle seems to cause stomach upsets in many people and is best removed. It grows under pines and is quite common.

Suillus grevillei (Klotzch) Singer [=*S. elegans*]
Cap: 5–15cm (2–6in)
Spores: 8–10 x 3–4μm
Edibility: edible but with caution; can cause upsets to some

This is perhaps our commonest species of *Suillus* in Britain and is very attractive with its bright yellow-orange cap and stem. The pores are yellow and bruise reddish-brown. The stem has a white, cottony ring at the top. In some areas, especially in Scotland, a deep reddish-chestnut form is found, but it agrees in all other essential details. This species is specific to larch and is found wherever this tree grows, often in a circle around it .

Suillus variegatus (Fries) Kuntze

Cap: 5–15cm (2–6in)

Spores: 7–10 x 3–5μm

Edibility: edible with caution; can cause upsets

This is something of an exception to the usual *Suillus* species in that it has a dry, woolly-velvety cap, but it is sticky below the woolly layer. The colour varies from pale yellow to orange-yellow. The pores are dark brownish-cinnamon. When cut the yellowish flesh turns a pale blue and has an acidic, fruity odour. One of the less common species, it is found under pines throughout Britain.

Suillus aeruginascens (Secretan) Snell

Cap: 5–10cm (2–4in)

Spores: 10–12 x 4–5μm

Edibility: edible but poor and may cause upsets

A contender for the title of the ugliest bolete, the cap is a dull, whitish-cream to dirty straw or olive with browner areas and streaks, and is soft and sticky. The pores are large, angular and olive-buff, bruising greenish-brown. The stem is straw yellow with a membranous ring. The flesh is creamy yellow flushed olive in the stem and staining blue-green in the stem base. Found only under larches, this rather uncommon species is widespread in Britain.

Suillus bovinus (Fries) Kuntze

Cap: 2.5–10cm (1–4in)

Spores: 8–10 x 3–4μm

Edibility: edible with caution; can cause upsets

One of the easiest ways to recognize this species is to turn it upside-down. The smooth, pinkish-clay to buff brown cap has a distinctly in-rolled whitish margin and the olive-buff to ochre pores have smaller pores within larger ones (referred to as compound pores). The short stem is minutely dotted at the apex and does not have a ring. This can be an abundant species under pines throughout Britain. It is widespread in the northern hemisphere, and is always associated with two-needled species of pines. A variety *viridocaerulescens* has been described, which turns faintly greenish-blue when cut.

Suillus cavipes (Opatowski) Smith & Thiers

Cap: 5–10cm (2–4in)
Spores: 7–10 x 3.5–4µm
Edibility: edible and quite good

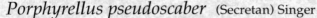

One of the dry, scaly species, this has an attractive reddish-brown to tawny cap. The specific name of *cavipes* refers to the usually hollow stem, which also has a white ring-zone at the apex. The pores are yellow, large and angular. Found only under larch, this is a rare species found mostly in the south.

Porphyrellus pseudoscaber (Secretan) Singer

Cap: 5–10cm (2–4in)
Spores: 10.5–18.5 x 5–7µm
Edibility: edible but very poor

The genus *Porphyrellus* is distinguished by its reddish-brown to purple-brown spores and its usually dull grey-brown colours. Many mycologists now treat it as a subdivision of the genus *Tylopilus*. This very uncommon species is a uniform dark grey-brown to black-brown on cap and stem, and the latter is quite smooth. The pores are a dingy olive-brown and bruise bluish or even reddish. It is widespread in Britain and found most often under conifers on acid soils. A second species, *P. porphyrosporus*, is often distinguished by its flesh turning blue-green and with very pale cream pores when young.

Strobilomyces floccopus (Fries) Karsten

Cap: 5–10cm (2–4in)
Spores: 10–12 x 8.5–11µm
Edibility: edible; looks rather unappealing when cooked but tastes quite good

It is a shame that this fascinating species is so rare in Britain, even though it is very widespread, having been found from Scotland down to the south of England. It represents the far-flung outrider of a large tropical group of boletes. If you head for Asia or Australia, or even North America, *Strobilomyces* species are very common. They all share very dark, blackish spores which are usually globose and ornamented with warts and ridges. This species has a shaggy-scaly black cap and stem with whitish-grey pores which bruise red. The flesh when cut stains deep orange-red then finally almost black. When cooked it turns quite black and looks very unappetizing. In Britain it is found in both deciduous and coniferous woods and can be considered a prize find on any fungal foray.

ORDER: RUSSULALES

Gilled mushrooms with flesh composed of groups of spherical cells (sphaerocysts) enclosed by long, cylindrical cells and with spores ornamented with amyloid warts or ridges. Consists of only one family.

RUSSULACEAE
Russula Family

In any walk through the woods the members of this family of mushrooms will form one of the most prominent and brightly coloured groups you will see. Although their identification can be very difficult and a matter for the specialist, there are, nevertheless, a number of species which have good distinguishing characteristics and can be tackled by the amateur. A number are also good edibles.

The two genera *Russula* and *Lactarius* are usually placed in their own order – the Russulales – because they differ so markedly from other gilled mushrooms. They have a characteristic brittle, crumbly texture in the hand, reflecting the unique cellular structure of their tissues, and their spores are ornamented with a variety of warts and ridges that stain blue-black when treated with a special iodine solution (Melzer's solution). Other important features are the taste of the cap flesh and gills, the odour, and the colour of the spore deposit. The latter is placed on a scale of pure white to ochre, designated by eight letters (A–H) shown below, and is vital to accurate identification, especially in *Russula*.

Lactarius differs from *Russula* in its usually duller colours and in its flesh which oozes a sticky latex when cut. This latex may be clear, white, or coloured. The spore colour is less variable in *Lactarius*.

Russula nigricans Fries

Cap: 5–15cm (2–6in)
Spores: white (A), 6–8 x 6–7μm, with a
fine network
Edibility: doubtful, best avoided

One of our commonest species. It is common in
many woodlands to come across circles of old
specimens looking as if they have all been burnt – a
result of the great colour change which takes place
as they mature. The cap starts white and rounded
but soon ages blackish-brown and becomes more
funnel shaped. The cap cuticle does not peel off
easily. The gills are very thick and very widely
spaced with a number of shorter, intermediate gills
present. The stem is short and firm, coloured like the
cap. The flesh is white, then soon red, and finally
black after cutting, and has a mild flavour.

Russula albonigra Fries

Cap: 5–10cm (2–4in)
Spores: white, (A–B), 7–10 x 6–7μm, with low
warts and a partial network
Edibility: inedible, best avoided

This and *R. nigricans* both blacken with age, but in
this instance there is no intermediate red stage and
there is often a striking contrast between the white
mushroom and its black stains. The gills are also
more crowded than in *R. nigricans* and the taste of
the flesh is odd with a menthol-like aftertaste. It is
not as common but is widespread in Britain under
beech and occasionally pine.

Russula delica Fries

Cap: 7.5–15cm (3–6in)
Spores: white to pale cream, (A–C), 8–10.5 x 6.5–
8.5μm with warts up to 1.7μm and a good network
Edibility: inedible

Often to be found bursting up through the leaf litter,
where it develops underground until it starts to
expand, this all-white species soon becomes funnel
shaped. The gills are crowded and sometimes have a
faint bluish tint. The taste varies from mild to quite
peppery in some forms. There is sometimes a thin
blue line at the top of the stem and this form is often
referred to as a separate species, *R. chloroides*.

Russula cyanoxantha Schaeffer ex Fries

Cap: 5–15cm (2–6in)
Spores: white, (A), 7–10 x 5.5–8μm, with small isolated warts
Edibility: edible and good

One of our commonest species, it is also something of a chameleon in its colour variations. It can be a mixture of lavender, green and purplish-brown or any one of these colours can predominate. Its most distinctive feature is the rather crowded white gills which are greasy and quite flexible to the touch, unlike almost all other species. Another unusual feature is the almost total lack of reaction to iron sulphate (FeSO₄); most species turn pink or green. The taste is mild to slightly peppery. The firm stem is white. It grows in mixed deciduous woods, especially beech and oak, sometimes under conifers.

Russula ionochlora Romagnesi

Cap: 5–10cm (2–4in)
Spores: pale cream (C), 6.5–7.5 x 5–6μm, with small isolated warts
Edibility: edible and quite good

The rather matt, dry cap is usually a mixture of lavender, grey and green or brown and any of these colours may dominate although lavender is the most common. The gills are pale cream and are brittle to the touch (compare with *R. cyanoxantha*). The stem is white and the taste is mild. FeSO₄ on the flesh turns pink. Often very common under oak and beech in parts of southern England.

Russula parazurea Schaeffer

Cap: 5–10cm (2–4in)
Spores: pale cream, (B–C), 6–8.5 x 5–6.5μm, with low warts and a fine network
Edibility: edible and quite good

A striking species with its grey-blue, grey-brown or lilac cap, usually strongly pruinose with a thick bloom like a grape, especially at the margin. The gills are pale cream and brittle. The stem is white or sometimes flushed violet. The flesh is mild to taste. Frequent under oaks and limes in England, this species is frequently confused with *R. cyanoxantha* but is easily distinguished by the cream spores and the pink reaction with FeSO₄.

Russula virescens (Schaeffer) Fries

Cap: 5–10cm (2–4in)

Spores: white, (A), 6–9 x 5.5–7μm, with isolated warts or sometimes with a few connecting lines

Edibility: edible and good

A beautiful species with the cap in delicate shades of grey-green, blue-green or yellowish-green, and easily distinguished by the cap surface which soon breaks up into fine flattened woolly patches. This can be an unusually firm and fleshy species as *Russula* species go, has a mild taste and is a popular edible in Europe. Unfortunately, it is equally attractive to the many fly larvae that like to infest mushrooms and it can be hard to find one that is untouched. It is widespread in Britain and grows under beech.

Russula aeruginea Lindblad

Cap: 5–10cm (2–4in)

Spores: deep cream (D–E), 6–10 x 5–7μm, with low warts and a few connecting lines

Edibility: edible

The genus *Russula* has a number of green species for the most part easily distinguished by either spore colour or other features of the cap. This species can be a bright grass-green or vary to a yellow-green, frequently with slight rusty spotting. The spores are a deep cream (D–E) compared with other green species such as *R. virescens* and *R. cyanoxantha,* which have white spores. Like them, it has a mild taste. This is a common species in mixed deciduous woods throughout Britain.

Russula emetica (Schaeffer) Persoon

Cap: 5–7.5cm (2–3in)

Spores: white (A), 7.5–12.5 x 6–9.5μm, with tall warts and a well-developed network

Edibility: inedible, very acrid and burning to taste

A widely illustrated and widely reported species, but it has also been a widely misidentified *Russula* in Britain. The true *R. emetica* is found in wet, boggy pine woods, frequently in *Sphagnum* moss. The cap is a brilliant scarlet to cherry-red, smooth and sticky when wet, and the cuticle can be completely peeled off when mature. The gills and stem are pure white, the stem often long and rather fragile. The taste is acrid and the odour is faint of fruit or coconut. The specific name refers to the fact that it can cause vomiting if eaten raw.

Russula mairei Singer
Cap: 5–10cm (2–4in)
Spores: white (A), 7–8 x 6–6.5µm, with medium warts in a well-developed network
Edibility: inedible, very acrid to taste

Frequently misidentified as *R. emetica* the bright red, rather matt cap may wash out after rain to a paler cream-pink, the cuticle peels almost entirely and very easily off the cap. The gills are white with a very faint blue-green hue when young, more cream with age. The stem is white, often rather short and the flesh is very acrid to taste. There is an odour rather like honey in older specimens. Very common under beech trees everywhere, never under pines.

Russula betularum Hora
Cap: 2.5–5cm (1–2in)
Spores: white (A), 8–10.5 x 6.5–8µm with warts connected by a partial network
Edibility: inedible, very acrid to taste

A pretty little species of the most delicate pastel pink fading to almost white; the cuticle peels almost completely. The gills and slender stem are snow white and the flesh has a fiercely hot taste. There is a delicate odour of coconut. This is widespread throughout Britain in damp birch woodlands but should be carefully compared with *R. fragilis* which grows in similar habitats and can also be pink in some of its colour forms.

Russula fragilis Fries
Cap: 1.5–5cm (½–2in)
Spores: white (A–B), 6–9 x 5–8µm, with a well developed network
Edibility: inedible, extremely acrid to taste

One of the commonest species of *Russula* in Britain it is also one of the most variable in colour, ranging from purple to red, or green or pink or almost black, or a mixture of all these. However, even in forms of a single colour the centre is usually greenish-grey to black. The gills are white and almost always minutely serrated along the edge (you may need a hand-lens for this). It can be found in both deciduous and coniferous woods throughout Britain.

Russula lutea (Hudson) Fries
Cap: 5–7.5cm (2–3in)
Spores: deep ochre(G–H), 7–9 x 6–8μm,
with rather tall, isolated warts
Edibility: edible

The sense of smell is very elusive and variable when tested across a range of people (and mushroom smells can be some of the most difficult to describe). This species has a very delicate and rather faint odour but most people relate it to fruit – peaches or apricots – or to honey as it gets older. It is the gills which give off most of the scent, and indeed this is true for most mushrooms. Apart from the odour it can be distinguished by its small, delicate caps, lovely rosy-peach to yellow coloration, and very deep ochre spores. The taste is mild. It is common under deciduous trees, especially beech, throughout England.

Russula puellaris Fries
Cap: 2.5–5cm (1–2in)
Spores: pale ochre (D–E), 6.5–9 x 5.5–7μm,
with rather tall, isolated warts
Edibility: edible but poor

Many *Russula* species change colour when bruised or with age and this species is easily distinguished by the deep ochre-yellow stains that appear over the entire mushroom in a few hours. The small, reddish-brown to purplish-brown cap is rarely seen without some yellow discoloration at the margin, and the gills and the soft, fragile stem usually look waterlogged and dull yellow. The taste is mild. A common species, it is found in rather wet areas of mixed woods throughout Britain.

Russula vinosa Lindblad [=R.obscura]
Cap: 5–12.5cm (2–5in)
Spores: medium ochre (D–E), 8–11 x 8–9μm,
with large, isolated warts
Edibility: edible and good

Another example of a species which changes colour, this very slowly turns ash-grey to blackish over a period of some hours. Scratching the stem is usually the easiest way to see the change, or it can be seen on the gill edges. The large cap is smooth, deep purple to wine-red, often depressed in the centre. The gills are broad, pale ochre. The tall, robust stem is white but also discolours grey-black as it ages, and if split open may be completely black inside. The taste is mild. A rather rare species, found in wet conifer woods, especially in Scotland.

Russula claroflava Grove

Cap: 5–10cm (2–4in)

Spores: pale ochre (E–F), 7.5–10 x 6–7.5μm, with more or less isolated warts

Edibility: edible and excellent

This species presents one of the brightest caps of any mushroom in the woods, the clear, vivid yellow colour being easily visible in the wet, boggy areas under birch where it grows. Like the previous species, however, it will slowly blacken over the course of a few hours, or in minutes if scratched. The broad gills are cream to pale ochre. It usually grows in *Sphagnum* moss and is found across the whole of the north temperate regions of the world. Despite its colour and blackening flesh it is an excellent edible mushroom.

Russula xerampelina (Schaeffer) Fries

[=*R. erythropoda*]

Cap: 5–10cm (2–4in)

Spores: pale ochre (E–F), 7.5–10 x 7–8.5μm, with tall isolated warts

Edibility: edible and good

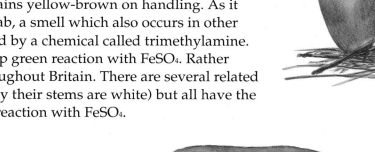

This mushroom has it all: beautiful colours, strange odour, colour-changing flesh and unusual chemical reactions. The cap is a deep purple to wine-red , sometimes almost black or olive-black at the centre, while the surface is dry and slightly wrinkled concentrically. The gills are pale ochre, while the stem is a beautiful purplish-red or pink but stains yellow-brown on handling. As it ages it smells strongly of old fish or crab, a smell which also occurs in other mushroom genera. The odour is caused by a chemical called trimethylamine. The taste is mild. The flesh gives a deep green reaction with $FeSO_4$. Rather uncommon; found in pine woods throughout Britain. There are several related species, differing in cap colour (usually their stems are white) but all have the fishy odour and all give a deep green reaction with $FeSO_4$.

Russula olivacea (Schaeffer) Fries

Cap: 10–15cm (4–6in)

Spores: deep ochre (G–H), 8–11 x 7–9μm, with very tall, isolated warts

Edibility: edible and excellent

This magnificent species rarely follows its specific name since it is most often deep purple in colour, not olive, although this colour can sometimes be found. There are often slight concentric bands apparent in the cap colour. The broad gills are deep ochre with the edges often marked in red. The robust stem is white flushed pink over the upper half and the flesh has a mild taste. It is found in Britain under beech trees and is, sadly, rather uncommon.

Russula atropurpurea Krombholtz

Cap: 5–10cm (2–4in)
Spores: white (A), 7–9.5 x 6–8μm, with a fine partial network
Edibility: edible but poor

The rich purple-red cap may be almost black at the centre and is sometimes irregularly blotched with paler areas. The cream gills are often spotted rust-red. The stem is white, sometimes flushed grey with age. The taste varies from mild to quite peppery. Very common in mixed woods, especially under oaks, throughout Britain. This name, although widely used, is unfortunately not valid under the rules of nomenclature, having been used earlier by someone else for a different mushroom, and must be changed. The most likely contender for a replacement may be *Russula vinacea* Burlingham, a species described from North America, which is identical to this one.

Russula caerulea Fries

Cap: 5–7.5cm (2–3in)
Spores: deep ochre (F–G), 8–10 x 7–9μm, with tall warts forming short ridges
Edibility: edible

One of the very few species with a distinctly umbonate cap, it is a deep purple-violet. The gills are broad and deep ochre when mature. The stem is white and club-shaped, while the flesh is white and mild to slightly bitter in taste. Quite common under pines throughout Britain.

Russula vesca Fries

Cap: 5–10cm (2–4in)
Spores: white (A–B), 6–8 x 5–6μm, with small warts, mostly isolated
Edibility: edible and quite good

Some cap colours can be very difficult to describe or characterize and this is certainly the case here. It varies from a pinkish-brown, through flesh tones or even slightly purplish, often unevenly coloured. Once you have seen a few specimens, however, it is actually quite distinctive. A good clue is to look closely at the cap margin (you may need a hand-lens) where the cuticle often retracts to expose the white flesh below. The gills are cream while the stem is white. FeSO$_4$ produces a deep salmon-brown reaction on the flesh. A common species found throughout Britain in mixed deciduous woods.

Russula amoena Quélet

Cap: 5–7.5cm (2–3in)

Spores: cream (B–C), 6–8 x 5.5–7μm, with short warts and a partial network

Edibility: edible

A beautiful, but sadly uncommon species, it exhibits a feature which is frequent in certain groups of *Russula* and indeed in other genera also. The cap surface is minutely velvety or matt and this texture is produced by thousands of microscopic finger-like cells standing up from the surface like a turf. The colours are rich reddish-purple to violet and both the stem and gill edges may be flushed with pinkish-purple. The flesh has an odd odour of Jerusalem artichokes. It is found mostly in southern England under beech.

Russula violeipes Quélet

Cap: 5–10cm (2–4in)

Spores: cream (B–C), 6.5–9 x 6.5–8μm, with low warts in a partial network

Edibility: edible

This species presents an unusual colour combination with a usually pale lemon cap contrasted against a purplish or violet flushed stem. This is variable, however, and the cap may also show some violet flushes. This is a firm species with a dry, matt cap and a slight odour of crab when old. It is quite common in some parts of southern England, usually found under beech or oak.

Russula laurocerasi Melzer

Cap: 5–10cm (2–4in)

Spores: cream (B–C), 7–8.5 x 6.5–7μm, with remarkably tall (2μm) ridges and flanges sticking out like wings

Edibility: inedible

Nowhere is the strangeness of some mushroom odours better demonstrated than in this species. It has the most wonderful smell of bitter almonds or marzipan as if it were a tempting confection. However, as it ages a sour undertone becomes more prominent in the smell and its taste can be quite hot and also unpleasant. The often very viscid cap is coarsely ridged and pimpled at the margin and both the cap and rather tall stem are a pale honey-brown. A much rarer species, *R. illota*, also has this odour but is distinguished by the violet-purple speckles over the gill edges and much shorter spore ornamentation. *R. laurocerasi* is sometimes quite common under oaks.

Russula foetens Fries
Cap: 7.5–15cm (3–6in)
Spores: cream (B–D), 8–10 x 7–9μm, with tall, isolated warts
Edibility: inedible

The specific name refers to the rather rancid, sour odour which soon develops, rather like a mixture of old cheese and oil. It is a large, rather ugly species with the tawny cap strongly ridged and pimpled at the margin. The taste is equally unpleasant being both hot, oily and sour. It can be found pushing up through the leaf litter and soil, often in large troops in mixed woods throughout Britain, but is rather erratic and only locally common.

Russula amoenolens Romagnesi
Cap: 5–10cm (2–4in)
Spores: cream (B–D), 6–9 x 5–7μm, with mostly isolated warts
Edibility: inedible

Perhaps our dullest species in appearance, the cap is in shades of drab brown and sepia, with strong marginal grooves and ridges. Combined with the fetid, cheesy odour and unpleasant, acrid taste, it has little to commend it. It can be a very common species in woods, parks and gardens under a variety of deciduous trees, often forming a circle around the base of the tree. It is widespread throughout Britain.

Russula farinipes Romell
Cap: 5–7.5cm (2–3in)
Spores: pure white, (A), 6–8 x 5–7μm, with isolated warts
Edibility: doubtful

Although this species belongs to the same group as the 'smelly' species described earlier (*R. foetens*, *R. amoenolens*), it is rather different in general appearance, being a much brighter colour and altogether more attractive in appearance. The ochre-yellow cap is matt with a tough, elastic cuticle, while the pale whitish-ochre stem is very mealy-granular on the upper half. The odour is slightly fruity and the taste is quite hot. It is quite uncommon and grows under deciduous trees on clay soils.

Russula fellea Fries

Cap: 5–10cm (2–4in)

Spores: cream (B–C), 7.5–9 x 5–6μm, with tall warts in a partial reticulum

Edibility: inedible

This common species could be called the Geranium Russula because of its distinctive odour of household geraniums (pelargoniums). Often abundant in the deep leaf litter of beech woods throughout Britain, it is of a uniform honey-yellow or ochre throughout. The taste is very acrid. The odour is best detected on the gills, although it must be said that a very small percentage of people seem to be completely unable to detect it.

Lactarius deliciosus (Fries) S. F. Gray – 'Saffron Milk Cap'

Cap: 5–10cm (2–4in)

Spores: cream 7–10 x 6–7μm, with a fine network

Edibility: edible and good

One of the brighter *Lactarius* species in this country, the bright orange, zonate caps stain or discolour slightly green with age. The stem is orange and frequently has small round pits or spots on the surface. When broken, the gills and flesh ooze an orange milk which hardly changes colour (note the difference from *L. deterrimus* description below). The taste of this latex and of the flesh is mild to slightly soapy and is considered good eating. It grows often in large numbers under pine throughout Britain. The equally common *L. deterrimus* is a lookalike which differs in its rapidly green-staining cap and gills, stem without pits and the latex changing to a dull wine-red in about 20–30 minutes. It is associated with spruce and is considered less tasty or even rather unpleasant to eat.

Lactarius salmonicolor Heim & Leclair

Cap: 5–10cm (2–4in)

Spores: cream, 9–12 x 6.5–7.5μm, with a partial network

Edibility: edible

A beautiful if rare species, the entire mushroom is a bright, clear orange without any green staining. The cap may be faintly zoned and the stem slightly pitted with darker spots. The latex is orange, becoming slowly reddish, and has a soapy, bitter flavour. It is associated with fir trees (*Abies* species) and seems to be most common in Scotland and in some arboretums in the south.

Lactarius turpis (Weinman) Fries
Cap: 7.5–15cm (3–5in)

Spores: cream, 6–8 x 5.5–6.5μm, banded with ridges

Edibility: inedible and very unpleasant

Perhaps the ugliest of *Lactarius* species, the roughened caps are deep olive-brown to blackish-green and often concentrically zoned with a paler, ochre margin. The gills are crowded and greenish-white, while the short stem is coloured like the cap and often pitted. The abundant latex is white, bitter and extremely unpleasant to taste. One of our commonest species, it occurs wherever there are birch trees and also sometimes pine. If a drop of ammonia is placed on the cap the reaction produces a deep violet stain.

Lactarius vietus (Fries) Fries
Cap: 2.5–8cm (1–3in)

Spores: cream, 7–8 x 5.5–6.5μm, with low warts in a partial network

Edibility: inedible

This is one of the *Lactarius* species whose latex discolours as it dries, and it is common to find specimens with their gills spotted with dark grey, although the latex is white when fresh. The entire mushroom is a uniform pale lilac-grey to brownish-grey with whitish gills. It is often very common and grows in wet, boggy places under birch, especially in *Sphagnum* moss. The taste of the latex is mild to slightly acrid.

Lactarius torminosus (Fries) S. F. Gray
Cap: 5–10cm (2–4in)

Spores: cream, 7.5–10 x 6–7.5μm, with a network

Edibility: inedible, often regarded as poisonous

When fresh and in good condition this can be one of the most spectacular species. The pink, zonate cap is remarkably shaggy-hairy all around the margin which starts off quite in-rolled. The gills are pinkish-white and the smooth stem is also pink. The white latex is copious when the flesh is broken and tastes painfully acrid and burning.It is frequent under birch throughout Britain. A closely related species – *L. pubescens* – is much paler, almost white, usually without any zones and less shaggy. It is uncommon but found in similar situations.

Lactarius helvus (Fries) Fries

Cap: 5–15cm (2–6in)

Spores: buff, 6–9 x 5.5–7.5μm, with mostly isolated warts

Edibility: inedible, perhaps poisonous

This is a large species with a remarkable odour, making it easy to identify in the field. The odour is variously described as resembling chicory, burnt sugar or curry powder, among others, but all agree it is spicy and quite pleasant. The cap is a pale cinnamon-brown, dry and slightly roughened. The latex is thin, watery and mild to taste. This is a fairly common species in mixed woods throughout Britain. There is much doubt as to the correctness of the name *helvus* and it seems likely that *L. aquifluus* is the correct name.

Lactarius rufus (Fries) Fries

Cap: 5–10cm (2–4in)

Spores: cream, 7.5–10.5 x 5–7.5μm

Edibility: inedible

This is a deceptive species as far as its taste is concerned and often catches out the unwary. Its white latex starts mild and only very slowly turns very acrid by which time it is too late to get rid of the taste. The cap is a deep fox-red to brick or bay and usually has a sharp, central knob or umbo. The stem is similarly coloured but has a whitish base. A very common species, it occurs in a variety of habitats in both pine and birch woods, but usually prefers boggy areas.

Lactarius volemus Fries

Cap: 5–10cm (2–4in)

Spores: 7.5–10μm, almost globose, with a fine network

Edibility: edible and good

Sadly, this beautiful species is rather rare in Britain, where it is usually found under oaks in the south. The rich, orange-brown cap and stem are dry and almost suede-like and usually have a characteristic puckered, wrinkled surface. The gills are cream and closely spaced. When any part of the mushroom is cut, a copious white, sticky latex oozes out, making it difficult to handle. It is thought that the latex in this and other species may act as a deterrent by glueing up the mouth parts of insect that like to feed on mushrooms. As the latex dries it discolours brown. The taste is quite mild and there is an odd odour of shrimp or shellfish when it is mature.

Lactarius pyrogalus (Persoon) Fries

Cap: 5–10cm (2–4in)

Spores: 6.5–7.5 x 5–6μm, with ridges and bands

Edibility: inedible; burningly hot to taste

The latin name *pyrogalus* translates as 'fire-milk' and a more apt description would be difficult to find. Anyone incautious enough to taste the latex in any quantity will discover the origin of the name and will certainly never forget the mushroom. The smooth cap is often zonate, ochre-brown to olive-ochre or greyish-ochre, as is the smooth stem. The gills are distinctive as they are rather widely spaced and a deep ochre-orange in colour. It is a common species and can be found under hornbeam and hazel throughout Britain.

Lactarius lignyotus Fries

Cap: 2.5–10cm (1–4in)

Spores: bright ochre, 9–10.5 x 9–10μm with a network

Edibility: edible

When fresh and young the surface of this mushroom looks like black velvet and it is one of the loveliest of the *Lactarius* species. It is also distinctive for the sharp umbo or point at the centre of the cap and for the contrasting white gills. To add to the exotic appearance the white, copious latex soon stains bright rose and the taste is peppery. Found under conifers, especially spruce, it is widespread but commonest in the north.

Lactarius camphoratus (Fries) Fries

Cap: 2.5–5cm (1–2in)

Spores: yellowish, 7–8.5 x 6–7.5μm, with a few connecting lines

Edibility: edible; makes quite a good spice when dried and ground

Although rather nondescript in appearance this is usually fairly easy to identify by the strong odour of curry powder, burnt sugar or chicory which develops with age. However, with experience one can learn to recognize it, even without the odour, as the cap and stem have a characteristic reddish-brown to liver colour and the cap has a small umbo at the centre. The latex is scanty, watery-white and mild to taste. A very common species, this is found in mixed woods throughout Britain.

Lactarius vellereus (Fries) Fries

Cap: 8–20cm (3–8in)

Spores: buff, 9–12 x 7.5–10μm, with very fine ridges

Edibility: inedible

Often forming huge fruit-bodies, this all-white to ivory species soon becomes deeply funnel shaped but the margin begins tightly rolled up and slowly unrolls. The stem is very short and hard, and like the cap is slightly velvety to the touch. The gills are fairly widely spaced and yellowish-cream. The latex is white, abundant and very acrid to taste. This is a common species and often bursts up through the leaf litter of the forest floor. A number of varieties or species have been separated out from this one, usually distinguished by differences in the reaction of the latex to KOH (supposedly none in the type species) and by the taste, whether very acrid or mild. For example, *L. bertillonii* has milk yellowing with KOH and a very slightly acrid taste.

Lactarius piperatus (Fries) S. F. Gray

Cap: 5–15cm (2–6in)

Spores: white, 6–8 x 5–5.5μm, with a faint network

Edibility: inedible, very acrid

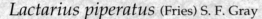

The gills of this species are so narrow and closely packed that it often seems to present an almost smooth surface on the underside of the cap. The entire mushroom is white and slightly velvety and soon becomes funnel shaped. The latex is white and copious and extremely acrid to taste and in some forms will dry an olive-green. A quite common species, it is frequent under deciduous trees throughout Britain and seems to prefer calcareous soils. The forms with latex turning green are often divided into two species, *L. pergamenus*, with gills not decurrent and rather rough cap surface, and *L. glaucescens*, with decurrent gills and smooth cap.

Lactarius tabidus Fries

Cap: 2.5–8cm (1–3in)

Spores: cream, 7–9 x 6–7.5µm, with tall ridges forming a partial network

Edibility: edible but of poor quality

This small, pinkish-brown to brick mushroom has a small, sharp umbo at the cap centre but is otherwise rather ordinary in appearance. Its most characteristic feature is the latex, which is white but slowly turns yellow if smeared on a handkerchief – but **not** if it stays on the gills. The latex is very scanty and is mild to taste. A very common species throughout Britain in mixed deciduous woods.

Lactarius chrysorrheus Fries

Cap: 2.5–8cm (1–3in)

Spores: pale yellow, 6–8 x 5.5–6.5µm, with isolated warts and a slight network

Edibility: edible but poor

A rather attractive species with a pale pinkish-cream to yellowish cap with noticeable concentric zones and/or watery spots. Like the previous species, this has latex which changes to yellow, but here the white latex is abundant and will stain bright yellow, even on the gills and cut flesh. The taste is quite mild. Another clue is that this species is only found growing under oak trees, where it forms a characteristic part of the oak flora in the autumn.

Lactarius glyciosmus (Fries) Fries

Cap: 2.5–8cm (1–3in)

Spores: cream, 6–8 x 5–6µm, with bands and ridges forming a broken network

Edibility: edible but poor quality

Mushroom odours can be quite amazing and some, as in this case, are very specific indeed. This species has a strong odour of desiccated coconut (not, it should be noted, of fresh coconut). The smell combined with the overall pale greyish-lavender colours make it easy to recognize. The latex is white, unchanging in colour and slightly acrid to taste. A common species in mixed woods throughout Britain. Despite the wonderful aroma, it is rather poor in flavour.

Lactarius blennius (Fries) Fries

Cap: 5–10cm (2–4in)

Spores: 7.5–8 x 5–6µm, with a partial network

Edibility: inedible

Often very viscid and glutinous, the olive-grey cap is usually marked with darker spots. The gills are crowded, white, and often spotted with grey. The latex is white, abundant and very acrid to taste and turns olive-grey as it dries. A common species, it grows under beech throughout Britain. A closely related species, *L. fluens*, is rather rare, but occurs under beech, usually on calcareous soils. It differs from *L. blennius* in its paler, greener, and more distinctly zonate cap, and its less viscid surface. It is also acrid to taste.

Lactarius quietus (Fries) Fries

Cap: 5–10cm (2–4in)

Spores: cream, 7–9 x 5.5–7µm, with mostly isolated warts and ridges

Edibility: inedible, very unpleasant

Walk through almost any oak wood in Britain and you are almost certain to find this species which only grows under oaks. Its dull, reddish-brown cap is zoned with darker bands and the white to yellowish-cream latex is mild then soon slightly acrid. It is the odour which characterizes it, however; it has a sweet, distinctly oily smell like some machine oils. A glance at any older mushroom literature will reveal descriptions of the odour as 'like bed bugs', but thankfully this is a smell less familiar, and therefore less useful to most people than it once was! The fungus has a mild but very disagreeable taste which renders it quite inedible.

ORDER: AGARICALES

An enormous group of fungi which share the common feature of having the spore-bearing basidia spread over thin gills (there are a very few exceptions which have developed without gills, just a smooth surface). They may have a central or oblique stem or have no stem at all and emerge directly from the substrate on which they grow. The tissues are almost entirely filamentous, except in the outer layers where globose cells may appear. The order is divided into a large number of families, often with very different spore colours.

HYGROPHORACEAE
Hygrophorus Family

All these mushrooms share the common character of thick, waxy gills and smooth, white spores formed on very long basidia. *Hygrophorus* species are usually thicker, fleshier and duller coloured than the fragile, often brilliantly coloured *Hygrocybe*.

Hygrocybe pratensis Persoon
Cap: 5–10cm (2–4in)
Spores: white, 6–7 x 4–5µm, smooth
Edibility: edible and quite good

As the cooler autumn days move in and the fields are soaked with rain, the species of *Hygrocybe* appear and this is one of the commonest and least brightly coloured of them. The flattened, top-shaped caps are a pale orange-buff and the gills run down the stem. It may also appear in grassy woodland clearings and garden lawns, and like most *Hygrocybe* species prefers a light, calcareous soil. A much paler, almost ivory or cream-coloured variety of this species – var. *pallida* – is often referred to as a separate species, *H. berkeleyi*, but the most recent monograph of the group does not consider the differences great enough to warrant this separation.

Hygrocybe virginea (von Wulfen ex Fries)
Orton & Watling [=H.niveus]

Cap: 2.5–5cm (1–2in)
Spores: white, 7–10 x 5–6µm, smooth
Edibility: edible

A number of white species have been described and are quite difficult to separate without a microscope, and even then not all experts agree on the names. Many mycologists consider *H. niveus* to be a good species in its own right. *H. virginea* is characterized by its smooth, slightly greasy and hygrophanous cap with a translucent, striate margin. The gills are distant and run down the stem. This is a common species of fields and pastures everywhere.

Hygrocybe conica (Scopoli) Kummer

Cap: 2.5–5cm (1–2in)
Spores: white, 8–12 x 5–7µm, smooth
Edibility: edibility uncertain; best avoided

A remarkable species which is also very attractive. The sharply conical cap is bright red while the tall, slender stem is yellowish, flushed red. The gills are pallid to yellowish. All parts bruise rapidly or age black and within a matter of hours the entire mushroom will look completely blackened. This is a common species in fields and grassy woodlands everywhere. Another species *H. pseudoconica* (=*H. nigrescens*) is often separated out by its more obtuse, blunt cap, larger and more robust fruit-bodies and four-spored basidia as against the usually two-spored basidia of *H. conica*. Many authorities consider them to be forms of one variable species.

Hygrocybe punicea (Fries) Kummer

Cap: 5–10cm (2–4in)
Spores: white, 8–11 x 5–6µm, smooth
Edibility: edible

A magnificent species, with a bright scarlet to blood-red cap and stem with a silky or greasy surface. The gills are yellowish to orange and only narrowly adnate, often with a slight decurrent tooth. Both the flesh and the base of the stem are whitish and this forms a key character of the species. Sadly, it is a rather uncommon species, found in fields and pastures throughout Britain. The closely related *H. coccinea* differs in being smaller and having reddish flesh and broadly adnate gills, but is otherwise similar in colour.

Hygrocybe miniata (Fries) Kummer
Cap: 2.5–5cm (1–2in)
Spores: white, 7–9.5 x 4–5.5µm, smooth
Edibility: edible

There are a number of small, bright red species, often quite difficult to separate, although by careful examination of some characteristics (a hand-lens is often required) several can be identified with reasonable accuracy. This species has a rough, scaly-squamulose cap surface with the scales often paler, yellower against the bright red background. The gills are broadly adnate with a small decurrent tooth and the flesh is odourless. The similar *H. strangulatus* has its spores slightly constricted, while *H. helobia* prefers moorlands rather than pastures. A common species, widespread through Britain.

Hygrocybe psittacina (Schaeffer ex Fries) Wünsche – 'Parrot Mushroom'
Cap: 1.5–2.5cm (½–1in)
Spores: white, 8–10 x 4–5µm, smooth
Edibility: edible

This species well deserves its common name of Parrot Mushroom since it is one of the few truly green fungi to be found, and like a parrot, can be a mixture of different shades mixed with yellow and orange, fading as it ages. The cap is smooth and viscid when wet and the gills are adnate, often with a notch where they join the stem (compare with *H. laeta*). A common species, especially later in the season, it occurs in grassy woodlands, fields and pastures everywhere.

Hygrocybe laeta (Persoon ex Fries) Kummer
Cap: 1–2.5cm (½–1in)
Spores: white, 5–7.5 x 4–5µm, smooth
Edibility: edible but worthless

This is often confused with *H. psittacina*, but there are some clear differences. The green tints in this species are confined to the gills and stem apex, while the cap is in shades of orange to olive-brown or orange-brown. The gills vary from whitish to olive to greyish-pink and are very broadly adnate to decurrent. The tall, slender stem is yellowish-green to greyish-orange. Both cap and stem are very slippery, glutinous when wet. A common species, it grows in pastures, fields and moors throughout Great Britain.

Hygrocybe unguinosa (Fries) Karsten
Cap: 2.5–5cm (1–2in)
Spores: white, 6–8 x 4–6μm, smooth
Edibility: edible

An unusual colour for a *Hygrocybe*, the grey to grey-brown cap and stem are both very glutinous and slippery and contrast with the white gills. The cap margin is often translucent-striate and the gills show through from below. A rather uncommon species in many areas, it grows, as do so many other *Hygrocybe* species, in fields and pastures.

Hygrocybe ovina (Bulliard ex Fries) Kühner
Cap: 2.5–7.5cm (1–3in)
Spores: white, 7–9 x 4.5–6μm, smooth
Edibility: edibility uncertain; best avoided

A very sombre-coloured member of this genus, the entire mushroom is a dark blackish-grey when moist, fading to grey-brown or buff when dry. All parts bruise red and then black when scratched or handled roughly and there is frequently an odour of ammonia or bleach, although this is sometimes absent. A very uncommon species, it grows in grassy deciduous woodlands, and is found mostly in the north of Britain.

Hygrophorus chrysodon (Batsch ex Fries) Fries
Cap: 2.5–7.5cm (1–3in)
Spores: white, 8–11 x 3.5–5μm, smooth
Edibility: edible

This is one of a number of white species of *Hygrophorus* to be found in woodlands, and is the easiest to distinguish by means of the bright golden-yellow flecks which dot the cap margin and stem apex. The cap is slimy-viscid when wet, as is the stem over its lower half. There is a distinct odour, said to resemble artichokes or bitter almonds. An uncommon species, it is widespread in woods of oak and beech throughout Britain. Also white and slimy is *H. eburneus*, found under beech. It is without yellow flecks, has an aromatic, sweet odour and turns yellow-ochre with caustic soda (KOH).

Hygrophorus penarius Fries
Cap: 5–10cm (2–4in)

Spores: white, 6–8.5 x 3–5μm, smooth

Edibility: edible

One of the larger and more robust of the white, woodland *Hygrophorus* species. The caps soon flatten out and have rather wavy, undulating edges and the gills are narrow, decurrent and pale cream in colour. The stem is stout and short. The cap and stem surface are quite dry to touch and have no particular odour. The similar *H. poetarum* usually has a brownish-yellow cap centre, a faint, fruity odour and larger, broader spores. *H. penarius* is a rare species found mainly in southern England under beech.

Hygrophorus russula (Schaeffer ex Fries) Quélet
Cap: 7.5–15cm (3–6in)

Spores: white, 6–8.5 x 4–6μm, smooth

Edibility: edible but sometimes bitter

A beautiful species with its large, whitish-pink caps mottled and spotted with dark wine-red blotches becoming totally reddish-purple with age, including the stem and the crowded gills. It is a robust, fleshy mushroom, often growing in large numbers or even in fairy rings in beech woods late in the year, but sadly is a rare species in this country. It prefers calcareous soils.

Hygrophorus hypothejus (Fries) Fries
Cap: 5–10cm (2–4in)

Spores: white, 8–9 x 4–5μm, smooth

Edibility: edible but poor

There are a number of species which appear very late in the year, just before the winter sets in, and which have a distinct veil on the stem. This species is very common and is distinguished by its glutinous, yellow-brown to olive-brown cap, whitish-yellow, decurrent gills and slender stem with a sticky coating below a faint ring zone. It grows under conifers and is widespread in Britain.

PLEUROTACEAE
Pleurotus Family

The genera which make up this family usually grow on wood and in the majority of species have the stem reduced or completely absent. The spores vary from white to pale lavender or even faintly pinkish. Some mycologists consider these to be closer to the tubed polypores rather than the other gilled mushrooms, and place them in the Polyporaceae family with the bracket fungi.

Pleurotus ostreatus (Jaquin ex Fries)
Kummer – 'Oyster Cap'
> **Cap**: 5–15cm (2–6in)
> **Spores**: pale lilac, 8–9 x 4–5µm, smooth
> **Edibility**: edible and considered a great delicacy

This well-known species is now such a popular edible it is cultivated commercially and is available from many greengrocers and specialist food stores. The caps usually have no stem but grow directly from the dead or dying timber and are a deep bluish-grey to grey-brown. The narrow, crowded gills are white to greyish and there is a pleasant odour. It grows, often in enormous numbers, late in the year from fallen or standing timber throughout Britain. The similar *P. pulmonarius* is usually almost white or cream and appears much earlier in the year. It is equally common and edible.

Pleurotus cornucopiae Paul ex Fries
[= *P. sapidus*]
> **Cap**: 5–15cm (2–6in)
> **Spores**: pale lilac, 8–11 x 3.5–5µm, smooth
> **Edibility**: edible and good

An unusual species, producing large clusters of fruit-bodies, often fused together. Each cap has a more or less central and quite well-developed stem. The gills are deeply decurrent and run down the funnel-shaped cap and stem. There is usually a delicate odour, like aniseed. A widespread species on fallen deciduous timber, it is regarded as edible but is perhaps not as well known as the Oyster Cap, *P. ostreatus.*

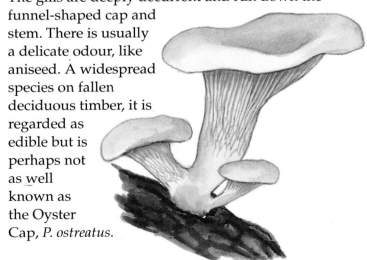

Phyllotopsis nidulans (Persoon ex Fries)
Singer
> **Cap**: 2.5–7.5cm (1–3in)
> **Spores**: pale yellowish-pink, 4–5 x 2–3µm, smooth
> **Edibility**: inedible

A striking species both in its colour – deep yellow-orange – and in its odour, which is rank and unpleasant, rather like rotted cabbage. The woolly surfaced, kidney-shaped cap has no stem and the bright yellow-orange gills are narrow and crowded. It grows on fallen timber of conifers and is uncommon in this country, usually seen late in the year, often in winter or through to early spring.

Panus tigrinus (Bulliard ex Fries) Singer
Cap: 2.5–7.5cm (1–3in)
Spores: white, 7–8 x 3–3.5μm
Edibility: edible but tough

The key characteristics of this species are the decurrent white gills with finely serrated edges, the slightly funnel-shaped cap, which is cream with fine brownish scales, and the almost central stem which is tough and fleshy. The spores are also distinctive, being very narrow, almost cylindrical. It is an uncommon species, preferring fallen timber of poplar and willow, and seems to be commonest in southern England.

Panellus serotinus (Hoffmann) Kühner
Cap: 5–10cm (2–4in)
Spores: yellowish, 4–6 x 1–2μm, smooth
Edibility: edible

This striking species is not often collected but this is mainly because it grows very late in the year when most mushroom hunters have stopped collecting until the coming spring. The semicircular caps are a deep olive-green to ochre-green, sometimes with a flush of violet, and the surface is decidedly velvety. The gills are crowded and pale yellow-orange. There may be a very short stem present. It is widespread in Britain on fallen timber.

Panellus stypticus (Bulliard) Karsten
Cap: 1–2.5cm (½–1in)
Spores: white, 3–5 x 1.5–3μm, smooth
Edibility: inedible

This small, rather inconspicuous mushroom is unusual in that it occurs in two forms depending on whether it is collected in Europe or in North America. The American form is brightly luminescent, the gills glowing yellow-green. Sadly, the European form is non-luminescent. The two forms will interbreed in culture, so are considered to be one species, although why such a striking difference should occur is uncertain. The shell-shaped cap is dull ochre-buff with a rough surface and a distinct but short stem is present at the trailing edge. The ochre-brown gills are crowded. The flesh is astringent and tastes very unpleasant. It is a common species on fallen timber everywhere, especially late in the year.

TRICHOLOMATACEAE
Tricholoma Family

This is an enormous family of mushrooms varying greatly in size and appearance and very difficult to define. Some have stems, some do not, some have even lost their gills and have a smooth undersurface. They all share white or at least very pale spores, some being yellowish or pinkish. The gills range from sinuate through adnate to decurrent but are never free. Many genera have some sort of veil present.

Omphalina pyxidata (Bulliard) Quélet
Cap: 0.6–2.5cm (¼–1in)
Spores: white, 7–10 x 4.5–6µm, smooth
Edibility: uncertain and in any case too small

This tiny, delicate species is common in grassy woodlands and lawns everywhere. The funnel-shaped cap is rusty-brown with a fluted margin. The decurrent gills are slightly paler, as is the rather short stem. This is one of a number of small species, varying in cap colour and other details which really require specialized literature to identify them. It may be considered typical.

Rickenella fibula (Bulliard ex Fries) Raith
Cap: 0.6–1cm (¼–½ in)
Spores: white, 4–5 x 2–2.5µm, smooth
Edibility: probably edible but too small

This species shows a definite preference for mossy areas in woods and fields. It can be quite a brightly coloured species, the cap orange-brown to reddish-brown with a striate margin. The gills are decurrent and widely spaced and a pale creamy-orange. The stem is usually long and slender. Once again, there are a number of similar species best distinguished with specialist literature, although most are not as brightly coloured as in this case.

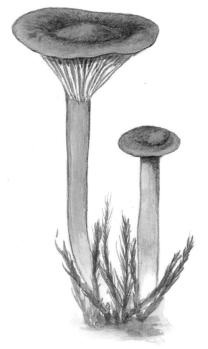

Cantharellula umbonata (Gmelin ex Fries) Singer
Cap: 2.5–5cm (1–2in)
Spores: white, 7–11 x 3–4µm, smooth
Edibility: doubtful; best avoided

Found in mossy areas on acid heath soils, this species is rather uncommon in Britain but is quite easy to recognize if close attention is paid to the gills, which are decurrent, thick, blunt-edged and are all forked one or more times. They may also spot reddish-brown on handling. The cap and stem are a dull grey-brown to blackish-grey, often with a lilac flush. The spores are unusual, being long and rather like those of a *Boletus* species in shape.

Xeromphalina campanella (Batsch ex Fries) Maire

Cap: 0.6–1cm (¼–½ in)

Spores: white, 5–8 x 3–4µm, smooth

Edibility: uncertain and too small anyway

Few fungi grow in such profusion as this species and to find a mossy stump covered with the great clumps and drifts of its orange caps is a beautiful sight. The tiny caps are depressed at the centre and the gills are decurrent. The thin stems are finely pubescent and very dark below. It is a typical feature of coniferous woods in Scotland and is rare elsewhere. Two other species (*X. cauticinalis* & *X. picta*) are described for Britain, and a couple more from mainland Europe, all would seem to be much rarer than *X. campanella,* although they are possibly under-recorded since the differences are often slight and need specialist literature for accurate identification. Their principal distinction from *X. campanella* is that they grow on the forest floor rather than on wood.

Armillaria mellea (Vahl ex Fries) Kummer – 'Honey Mushroom'

Cap: 5–10cm (2–4in)

Spores: white, 7–10 x 5–6µm, smooth

Edibility: edible, but must be well cooked; considered a great delicacy

Formerly considered a very variable species, it has in recent years been split into a number of different species, some of which are easily distinguished. This species is a serious parasite of woodland trees and plantations and causes many millions of pounds' worth of damage every year the world over. It will also attack a very large array of other plants in woods and gardens, including many popular shrubs. The caps are almost smooth and vary from bright honey-yellow to greenish-yellow with a darker centre, where there are minute brownish scales. The stems taper downwards and are fused together to form large clumps. There is a well-developed woolly ring above, white to yellow. If the bark of the dead or dying tree on which it appears is peeled back, long, very tough black 'bootlaces' may be found. These rhizomorphs are the Honey Mushroom's way of spreading long distances to infect other trees.

Armillaria lutea Gillet – 'Honey Mushroom'
[=A.bulbosa]
> **Cap**: 5–10cm (2–4in)
> **Spores**: white, 7.5–8.5 x 4.5–5µm, smooth
> **Edibility**: edible and excellent when well cooked

The earlier synonym of *A. bulbosa* actually describes this species well. The stems are indeed bulbous, never tapered as in the previous species. The caps are reddish-brown to pinkish-brown with darker brown scales at the centre. The gills are cream, to pinkish-buff. The stems are pinkish-buff to cream often with a yellow coating at the base. A key character is the white, cobwebby veil at the stem apex, unlike the thick woolly ring of *A. mellea*. Also unlike *A. mellea*, this species rarely grows in clumps but is usually scattered singly over a wide area and is very often found on the ground, presumably arising from buried wood or tree roots. *A. cepistipes* is a species so similar to this one that it is almost impossible to distinguish without detailed microscopic examination, and for most purposes may be considered the same.

Armillaria ostoyae Romagnesi – 'Honey Mushroom'
> **Cap**: 5–10cm (2–4in)
> **Spores**: white, 8–10 x 5–6µm, smooth
> **Edibility**: edible when well cooked

This is the scaliest of the species, with the dark reddish-brown caps having dark blackish-brown scales. The stems are even to club-shaped and it grows in small to large clumps on stumps and at the base of trees. The ring is white, very distinct with dark blackish-brown scales on the edge, below and also down the stem in many specimens.

Armillaria tabescens (Scopoli ex Fries) – Emel 'Honey Mushroom'
> **Cap**: 5–7.5cm (2–3in)
> **Spores**: white, 8–10 x 5–7µm, smooth
> **Edibility**: edible and good when well cooked

This Honey Mushroom is the exception to the rule. Although it is very similar in general appearance to the other species, it is completely without any trace of a veil or ring on the stem. The yellow-brown caps are smooth with minute brown scales at the centre. The gills are adnate to slightly decurrent and pale buff. The slender stems are fused at the base to form often huge clumps. It is erratic in the times it appears, seeming to prefer years with hot summers, and after which it may not be seen for several seasons. It grows at the base of various deciduous trees, especially oaks, and is a serious parasite in some areas.

Hygrophoropsis aurantiaca (von Wulfen ex Fries) Maire – 'False Chanterelle'

Cap: 2.5–7.5cm (1–3in)

Spores: white, 5–8 x 3–4.5μm, smooth

Edibility: often thought to be poisonous, but apparently it is just tasteless

As the common name of False Chantarelle suggests, it can be confused with the genuine Chanterelle, *Cantharellus cibarius*, but it differs in a number of respects. The soft, slight velvety yellow-orange cap is thin-fleshed and has an in-rolled margin. The gills (it has true gills, unlike the genuine Chanterelle) are thick and blunt-edged, fork repeatedly and are a bright yellow-orange. The stem is slender and yellow. The true affinities of this mushroom probably lie with *Paxillus* in the Paxillaceae family, since they share many features, except for the spore colour, but it is placed here in its traditional position because most people will expect to look for it among other white-spored mushrooms. It is very common in mixed woods and heaths throughout Britain.

Clitocybe clavipes (Persoon ex Fries) Kummer

Cap: 5–7.5cm (2–3in)

Spores: white, 6–8.5 x 3–5μm, smooth

Edibility: suspect; has been reported to cause nausea when consumed with alcohol

This common species is quite attractive in a subdued sort of way, the slightly domed, grey-brown to ochre-brown cap contrasting with the pale yellow-cream decurrent gills. The grey-brown stem swells out below very much like a club (*clavipes* is Latin for club-foot). There is a faint, delicate but very sweet odour present like spice or flowers. The reported reaction with alcohol is something which also turns up in other, unrelated mushrooms. It consists of palpitations, flushing and nausea. A common species of pine woods everywhere.

Clitocybe geotropa (Bulliard ex Fries) Quélet

Cap: 5–20cm (2–8in)

Spores: white, 6–7 x 5–6μm, smooth

Edibility: edible but perhaps best avoided in case of confusion with other white species which are poisonous

This can be a very large and stately mushroom with a funnel-shaped cap, usually with a central umbo. The colour ranges from white to ivory or pale buff. The decurrent gills are white and quite crowded. The stem is tall and firm. It often grows in small troops under deciduous trees and seems to prefer calcareous soils.

Clitocybe gibba (Persoon ex Fries) Kummer
[=*C. infundibuliformis*]
Cap: 5–10cm (2–4in)
Spores: white, 5–8 x 3.5–5µm, smooth
Edibility: edible but not recommended

One of the commonest species of *Clitocybe*, the delicate pinkish-buff to tan cap is very thin-fleshed and soon funnel shaped. The crowded gills are whitish and decurrent and the stem is slender and whitish. There is a pleasant, fragrant odour, a little like almond or anise. It grows in both conifer and deciduous woods and is found throughout Britain.

Clitocybe nebularis (Batsch) Kummer
Cap: 5–15cm (2–6in)
Spores: pale buff, 6–7 x 3–4µm, smooth
Edibility: edible with caution; has caused upsets to some; best avoided

Sometimes given the common name of Clouded Agaric, this refers to the cap colour, which is a smoky grey-brown. The cap is large and smooth, with a central dome or boss, while the gills are slightly decurrent, crowded and pale cream. The stout stem is rather short and fibrous, grey like the cap. It grows late in the year, often during the first frosts, and may appear in large fairy rings. It prefers deep leaf litter or compost and frequently appears in gardens.

Clitocybe odora (Bulliard ex Fries) Kummer
Cap: 2.5–7.5cm (1–3in)
Spores: pinkish–buff, 6–7 x 3–4µm, smooth
Edibility: edible and quite good

This species has one of the loveliest odours in the mushroom world, smelling exactly like fresh anise extract, and can often be detected in the woods from some distance away. Combined with the delicate blue-green coloration of the slender fruit-body, it forms one of the most recognizable of species. Added to this is the rather unusual spore colour. All told, these characteristics make it an easy species for the beginner to identify. Fortunately, it is a common species in woods everywhere.

Clitocybe rivulosa (Persoon ex Fries) Kummer

Cap: 2.5–5cm (1–2in)
Spores: white, 4–5.5 x 2.5–3μm, smooth
Edibility: extremely poisonous

This is one of a number of small white species of *Clitocybe* and they can be very difficult to distinguish accurately. They should certainly all be avoided as far as eating is concerned. This one has a 'frosty' coating which is usually cracked in concentric zones, showing a browner undersurface. The gills are crowded, white and adnate. It grows in open grass, often in circles, late in the year. It contains large amounts of the toxin muscarine, which can cause death in large quantities. There is some difference of opinion as to the correct name for this species and it may be that *C. dealbata* should be used.

Clitocybe nuda (Bulliard ex Fries) Bigelow & Smith – 'Wood Blewit' [=*Lepista nuda*]

Cap: 5–15cm (2–6in)
Spores: pale pinkish-buff, 6–8 x 4–5μm, minutely roughened
Edibility: edible and good and very popular

This species is usually placed in the genus *Lepista*, which is characterized by its roughened, pinkish spores, but many mycologists feel that the two genera merge gently into each other with no clear demarcation, so they group them all under *Clitocybe*, as is done here. This common species is to be found in large numbers, often in rings at the end of the year. It is very characteristic with its deep violet cap, gills and stem, although the cap soon fades to brownish with age. It has a very pleasant, flowery-fruity odour and mild taste, and is widely collected for eating. It might be confused with some of the violet-purple *Cortinarius* species but these all have rust-brown spores.

Clitocybe inversa Scopoli ex Fries

Cap: 5–10cm (2–4in)
Spores: pale creamy-yellow, 4–5 x 3–4μm, minutely roughened
Edibility: edible but not recommended

The funnel-shaped cap is a rich tawny to foxy-red fading to pale orange-brown with age and when dry. The gills are crowded and decurrent. The stem is slender and quite tall. It often grows in troops in deep leaf litter of both deciduous and coniferous trees from late summer onwards. Because of the coloured, roughened spores it is often placed in the genus *Lepista*, but that genus is here included under the concept of *Clitocybe*.

Laccaria laccata (Scopoli ex Fries) Berkley & Broom

Cap: 1–5cm (½–2in)
Spores: white, 7–8μm, subglobose with spines up to 1μm
Edibility: edible

One of the commonest of fungi and distributed across most of the temperate parts of the world. It is also one of the most variable, with numerous varieties, subspecies or even species being separated out by different authorities. The basic characters include the reddish-brown to pinkish-brown cap, which may be slightly scurfy at the centre, and the thick, pale pinkish-brown gills. The stem is slender, fibrous and reddish-brown. It grows in all sorts of woodlands, especially along paths and woodland edges, but also in open heaths with scattered trees.

Laccaria bicolor (Maire) Orton

Cap: 2.5–5cm (1–2in)
Spores: white, 7–9 x 6.5–7μm, with sharp spines up to 1μm
Edibility: edible

At first sight it looks much like other *Laccaria* species, with a reddish-brown to pinkish-brown cap and stem, but a closer examination will reveal that the gills are a bright pinkish-lilac and the base of the stem has a bright lilac-violet woolly coating. It is not as common as *L. laccata* but is likewise widespread and grows in a wide variety of habitats, including mossy pathsides.

Laccaria amethystea (Bulliard) Murrill

Cap: 2.5–5cm (1–2in)
Spores: white, 8–10μm, globose with minute spines
Edibility: edible

One of the most beautiful of all fungi. When fresh and moist the entire fruiting body is a deep, intense amethyst-violet. As it dries, however, the cap fades to a dull greyish-lilac, although the gills usually retain their deep violet hue. This is a common species but seems to prefer shadier, moister areas of woodland than such species as *L. laccata*, and is found throughout Britain.

Laccaria proxima (Boudier) Patouillard

Cap: 2.5–7.5cm (1–3in)
Spores: white, 7.5–10 x 6.5–7μm, with spines
up to 1.5μm
Edibility: edible

Our largest and tallest species of *Laccaria,* it seems to prefer more open woods or moorland and is often found in *Sphagnum* moss. The cap is finely scaly, reddish-brown and the gills are thick, widely spaced and pinkish. The tall stem is very fibrous to slightly scaly and coloured like the cap. The size of all *Laccaria* species can vary, so the spore shape and size, as well as the number of spores on the basidium, are important characters. It is quite common and widespread in Britain.

Laccaria tortilis (Bolton) S. F. Gray

Cap: 0.6–1cm (¼–½ in)
Spores: white, globose, 11–16μm and spiny,
with only two spores per basidium
Edibility: edible but too small

Probably our smallest species, it is striking for its very thick and very sparse gills, and for the wavy-fluted cap which is pale pinkish. This is a very uncommon species, although it is also probably overlooked because of its small size. It prefers very damp areas, often bare soil in deep shade, such as stream sides and banks or deep, shady tracks in woodlands.

Tricholoma sulphureum (Bulliard ex Fries) Kummer

Cap: 5–10cm (2–4in)
Spores: white, 9–12 x 5–6μm, smooth
Edibility: inedible, possibly poisonous

This is a good example of just how powerful (and unpleasant) some mushroom odours can get. The fungus gives off a strong, penetrating odour of coal gas that can be smelled from some distance away. Combined with the overall bright sulphur-yellow to ochre-yellow colours, it forms an easily recognizable mushroom. It is quite common, especially late in the season under oaks and beeches on acid soils.

Tricholoma saponaceum (Fries) Kummer

Cap: 5–10cm (2–4in)

Spores: white, 5–6 x 3.5–4μm, smooth

Edibility: inedible, possibly poisonous

A very variable mushroom both in colour and in smell (on which there is some disagreement), but the basic colours are greenish-grey to grey-brown, often with pink flushes in the stem base and gills. The cap is smooth to minutely scaly. The odour is variously described as rather fragrant, of soap or flowers, or sour like sesame oil, or of green almonds. It is a common species in mixed woodlands, particularly on clay soils.

Tricholoma sulphurescens Bresadola

Cap: 5–10cm (2–4in)

Spores: white, 5–6 x 4–5μm, smooth

Edibility: inedible

A very rare species, it is nevertheless quite easy to identify. The entire fruiting body is white to cream and all parts rapidly stain sulphur-yellow if handled or bruised. The odour is rank and unpleasant when old, although the taste is quite mild. The cap is smooth and silky to touch and the gills are narrow and crowded with rather wavy edges. The stem is firm and fleshy, quite fibrous and rather rooting. Its distribution is uncertain because of its rarity, but it occurs under oaks and conifers.

Tricholoma terreum (Schaeffer) Kummer

Cap: 5–10cm (2–4in)

Spores: white, 5–7 x 4–5μm, smooth

Edibility: edibility uncertain, best avoided

There are a number of grey *Tricholoma* species, not all easy to distinguish. Close attention must be paid to such characteristics as taste, texture of cap surface, and colour of gill edges. The species shown here has a felty-tomentose grey to grey-brown cap. The gills are broad, grey-white, notched where they join the stem. The short stem is white, smooth. It has a mild taste and is almost odourless. It often grows in large troops and is found under pines late in the season throughout Britain.

Tricholoma virgatum (Fries) Kummer

Cap: 5–10cm (2–4in)

Spores: white, 6–7 x 5–6μm, smooth

Edibility: usually considered inedible

This is one of a few species with a peppery or burning taste to the gills and flesh. The cap is almost conical and is grey to grey-black with darker greyish fibres, and is almost smooth to silky to touch. The gills are broad, white and notched by the stem. The stem is white and rather tall, firm and smooth. It grows in small troops under conifers throughout Britain.

Tricholoma columbetta (Fries) Kummer

Cap: 5–10cm (2–4in)

Spores: white, 5–7 x 3.5–4.5μm, smooth

Edibility: inedible

A striking, beautiful species, it is distinguished by its snow-white cap, gills and stem, becoming slightly buffy at the cap centre with age. An unusual phenomenon is the appearance of tiny red or blue-green spots scattered over the fruiting body. It is not known for certain what causes them and not all specimens are affected, but it has been suggested that they may be bacterial in origin. Other white species usually have a distinct, strong odour or stain when bruised. This species grows under mixed deciduous trees and seems to prefer neutral to alkaline soils.

Tricholoma sejunctum (Sowerby ex Fries) Quélet

Cap: 5–10cm (2–4in)

Spores: white, 5–6 x 4–5μm, smooth

Edibility: inedible

A very variable species. A number of different varieties have been described, based mainly on colour or habitat differences. The commonest forms are yellow-green to olive-grey in colour with darker radiating fibrils, browner at the centre. Some forms are browner or greener, others are much paler, almost yellow. The gills are white to yellowish, broad and crowded with a notch by the stem. The stem is firm, stout and white to flushed slightly yellowish or green. The odour and taste are strong of meal or flour becoming rather bitter. It is a common species in both coniferous and deciduous woods throughout Britain. The similar *T. luridum* has dark grey-black fibrils, greyish-white gills and spores up to 7.5μm long. It grows in similar habitats.

Tricholoma flavovirens (Persoon ex Fries)
Lundell [=*T. equestre*]
> **Cap**: 5–10cm (2–4in)
> **Spores**: white, 6–8 x 3–5µm, smooth
> **Edibility**: edible and good

An attractive species and quite variable, depending upon habitat. The cap is usually broadly bell-shaped, the top flattened, smooth, yellow-brown to brownish-olive with darker brown squamules. The gills are bright yellow, crowded and notched by the stem. The stocky stem is brownish-yellow, paler above, although the flesh inside is white. The odour is mealy, as is the taste. It is found mainly under pines on sandy soils and is widely distributed. It is one of the few species considered to be a good edible.

Tricholoma portentosum (Fries) Quélet
> **Cap**: 5–12.5cm (2–5in)
> **Spores**: white, 5–6 x 3.5–5µm, smooth
> **Edibility**: edible and good but confusion with other species is possible

The characteristic of this species is the yellow flush which spreads over the stem and gills, and the blunt, grey-brown cap which is streaked with darker fibrils. There may also be greenish or even violet tones present. The stem is usually large and stout. It usually appears very late in the season often growing in rings or troops under pines or beech, most commonly in Scotland.

Tricholoma fulvum (A. P. de Candolle)
Saccardo
> **Cap**: 5–10cm (2–4in)
> **Spores**: white, 5–7 x 3–4.5µm, smooth
> **Edibility**: inedible

This is perhaps one of the easier species to identify once the key features are understood. Although there are other reddish-brown species, this one is unique in its yellowish, brown-spotted gills and yellow flesh in the stem, easily seen by gently splitting the stem with a fingernail. The cap is sticky when wet and has a grooved margin, but is otherwise smooth. It is one of our commonest species and grows exclusively under birch in boggy situations, appearing rather earlier than most other *Tricholoma* species. Another species – *T. nictitans* – is sometimes separated out. It differs in growing under pines and in having pallid, not yellow, gills and a smooth, not grooved, margin.

Tricholoma aurantium (Schaeffer ex Fries) Ricken

Cap: 5–10cm (2–4in)
Spores: white, 4–5 x 3–3.5μm, smooth
Edibility: inedible

Rather brightly coloured for a *Tricholoma*, this attractive species is a bright orange to orange-brown with a viscid cap contrasting against the almost white gills. The latter are often spotted with reddish-brown. The stem is similarly coloured, with irregular zones up to a distinct ring-zone; it is white above. The taste and odour are mealy or cucumber-like. In Britain it is confined mostly to the Scottish Highlands under pines.

Tricholoma caligatum (Viviani) Ricken
[=*Armillaria caligatum*]

Cap: 5–15cm (2–6in)
Spores: white, 6–7.5 x 4.5–5.5μm, smooth
Edibility: edible but poor

There is a group of *Tricholoma* species where the veil is well developed and forms a ring and/or scaly zones on the stems. Because of this many of them were formerly placed in the genus *Armillaria,* but in other respects they are typical of *Tricholoma*. This species is large, rather dull in colour, with darker scales on the pallid cap. The stem is white with a sheath of brown scales, patches and zones over the lower half. There may be bluish-grey tones present in some forms. It is an uncommon species found mainly in Scotland under pines, often in very large numbers.

Leucopaxillus giganteus (Fries) Singer

Cap: 10–40cm (4–16in)
Spores: cream, 6–8 x 4–5.5μm, amyloid
Edibility: edible.

This enormous species can be quite spectacular when found growing in the large fairy rings that it forms. The white to buff cap is soon funnel shaped, with an in-rolled, grooved margin, and has a suede-like texture. The crowded, narrow gills are decurrent down the short, stout stem. It prefers open meadows or woodland clearings and although uncommon it is quite widespread. *Leucopaxillus* species are among a number of fungi which yield useful chemicals: this species provides an antibiotic called clitocybin.

Melanoleuca melaleuca (Persoon ex Fries) Maire

Cap: 5–10cm (2–4in)

Spores: white, 7–8.5 x 5–5.5µm, amyloid and minutely warted

Edibility: edibility uncertain; best avoided

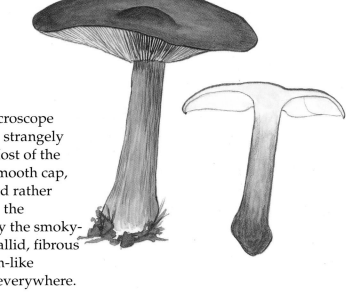

This is a group of fungi which provide a good reason to use a microscope since many of the species have fascinating cells on the gills, often strangely shaped like harpoons or clubs, and quite beautiful to examine. Most of the species have a characteristic bump or umbo at the centre of the smooth cap, and a fibrous stem. The species are variable in their characters and rather difficult to distinguish. Certainly there seem to be more names in the literature than there are good species. This one is characterized by the smoky-brown to dark brown cap with white, sinuate gills. The stem is pallid, fibrous and the flesh is often browner in the base. It has pointed, harpoon-like cystidia. It is common and grows in mixed woods and clearings everywhere.

Melanoleuca cognata (Fries) Konrad & Maublanc

Cap: 5–10cm (2–4in)

Spores: unusual for the genus, deep creamy yellow, 9–10 x 6–7µm, with amyloid warts

Edibility: edible

This is one of the easier species to identify because of the bright ochre-yellow colours of the cap, floury-rancid odour, rather short, stout stem and the deep creamy-yellow spores (most *Melanoleuca* spores are white to cream). It is fairly common, preferring open woodlands or even pastures and is widely distributed. This may be one of a complex of very closely related forms since there are discrepancies in the literature as regards cap colour and spore colour.

Lyophyllum decastes (Fries) Singer

Cap: 5–10cm (2–4in)

Spores: white, globose, 4-6µm, smooth

Edibility: edible and good

Enormous clumps of this mushroom can be found bursting up through soil or gravel or even through tarmacadam. It seems to show a definite preference for roadsides or trackways or other disturbed areas. The caps vary greatly in colour from grey to brown and are smooth and dry to touch. The stout, firm stems are white and smooth. A number of other forms (or species) have been described but since many of the characters seem to intergrade they seem of doubtful value. In North America this is often called the Fried Chicken Mushroom because of the taste, and I would agree that it is one of the best mushrooms I have tried for both flavour and texture.

Calocybe gambosum (Fries) Donk –
'St George's Mushroom' [=*Tricholoma gambosum*, =*T. georgii*]

Cap: 5–15cm (2–6in)
Spores: cream, 4–6 x 2–3.5μm, smooth
Edibility: edible and good

The common name, St George's Mushroom, reflects the time of fruiting, since it appears around mid-April (St George's day is 26 April), and fruits through May to early June. The only other large mushrooms which might be found in the spring are some species of *Entoloma;* these are easily distinguished by their pink, angular spores. *C. gambosum* is a uniform cream to ivory with a heavy, fleshy cap and stem and crowded, narrow gills, usually notched at the stem. The flesh has a strong odour and taste of meal or cucumber. It often grows in large fairy rings and prefers grassy woodlands or hedgerows and is common almost everywhere. It is a good edible, although the mealy flavour is an acquired taste for some.

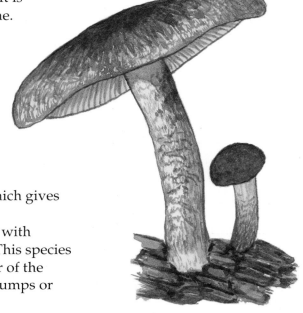

Tricholomopsis rutilans (Schaeffer ex Fries)
Singer

Cap: 5–15cm (2–6in)
Spores: white, 7–8 x 5–6μm, smooth
Edibility: edible but poor

This is sometimes given the common name of Plums and Custard, which gives an accurate idea of the colours present in this species. It is a beautiful combination of wine-red tiny scales overlaying a yellow background, with bright golden-yellow gills–altogether an unmistakable combination. This species is an example of why you should not judge spore colour by the colour of the gills; in this instance you will be misled. It grows on or near conifer stumps or sawdust and is common throughout Britain.

Megacollybia platyphylla (Persoon ex Fries)
Kotlaba & Pouzar [=*Tricholomopsis platyphylla*]

Cap: 5–15cm (2–6in)
Spores: white, 7–9 x 5–7μm, smooth
Edibility: inedible

This is one of the earliest mushrooms to appear, following late-spring rains and continuing to fruit throughout the summer and early autumn. Its cap is a dull grey to grey-brown, smooth with fine radiating fibres. The gills are the most recognizable feature, however, being white, very broad and widely spaced, with the edges often split or jagged and with a notch where they join the stem. The stem is white and firm, then hollow, soft and very fibrous, and if carefully traced down into the wood or soil will be seen to form long, white mycelial strands at the base. Extremely common, it is sometimes the only species fruiting in a woodland in summer and grows from logs, stumps or buried wood.

Asterophora lycoperdoides (Bulliard ex Mérat) Ditmar

Cap: 0.6–2cm (¼–¾ in)
Spores: basidiospores white, 3.2–5.8 x 2.0–4.2μm, chlamydospores 13–20 x 10–20μm, strongly warted and bluntly spiny
Edibility: unknown; too small

Here is a fungus attacking a fungus. This strange organism is only found on mushrooms of the genera *Russula* and *Lactarius*, and they have to be old and rotting specimens at that. The small caps are squat and misshapen and are soon covered in a thick, brownish powder. This is a layer of thick-walled asexual spores called chlamydospores which are completely separate from the normal basidiospores produced on the rudimentary gills. It is widespread, although seldom common, and seems to prefer very wet years. The similar *A. parasitica* also grows on rotting *Russula* and *Lactarius* but differs in the more perfect caps, well-formed gills and lack of brown chlamydospores.

Flammulina velutipes (Fries) Karsten

Cap: 2.5–7.5cm (1–3in)
Spores: white, 7–9 x 3–6μm, smooth
Edibility: edible and good

Very few mushrooms can withstand frosts or even cold weather for a prolonged period, but this species is actually stimulated into growth and fruiting by such temperatures. It starts to fruit around October and goes right through to the early spring, and can often be picked in December and January. The bright orange-yellow to orange-brown caps are smooth and sticky, while the gills are pale creamy yellow. The slender stems are velvety and yellow, becoming deep blackish-brown below. It grows in clumps on dead or dying deciduous timber throughout Britain.

Cystoderma terrei (Berkeley & Broom) Harmaja [=C. cinnabarinum]

Cap: 2.5–7.5cm (1–3in)
Spores: white, 3.5–5 x 2.5–3μm, smooth
Edibility: inedible

An uncommon species, but quite beautiful with its rich brick-red to orange cap and stem and powdery-granular surface. The gills are white, as is the apex of the stem above a distinct ring-zone. It grows in mixed woods, often under conifers, and is widespread in Britain. There is some uncertainty as to where *Cystoderma* should be placed. Some mycologists put it close to *Tricholoma* as here; others believe it to be related to *Lepiota*.

Cystoderma amianthinum (Scopoli) Fayod

Cap: 2.5–5cm (1–2in)

Spores: white, 4–6 x 3–4μm, smooth

Edibility: inedible

The powdery-granular cap is bright yellow-ochre and usually wrinkled at the centre. The stem has a yellow, granular coating up to a slight ring-zone near the apex. The gills are white to cream. This is the commonest species in the genus and grows in conifer woods throughout Britain.

Xerula radicata (Relhan ex Fries) Dörfelt

[=*Oudemansiella radicata*]

Cap: 5–12.5cm (2–5in)

Spores: white, 12–18 x 9–12μm, smooth

Edibility: inedible

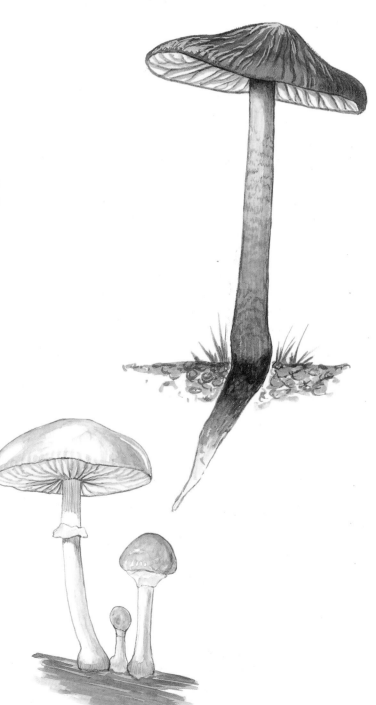

Many fungi seem to prefer to grow from buried wood or tree roots rather than on wood lying on the surface and these species often develop long mycelial strands to penetrate the soil. Nowhere is this more developed or so spectacular as in this species. The stem is prolonged into a long, deeply rooting 'taproot' which can be traced down to 20cm (8in) or more in some specimens. The ochre-brown to buff cap is viscid in wet weather and often extremely wrinkled and veined. The gills are white, very broad and widely spaced. The stem is tough, smooth and white to finely brown scurfy-floccose below. The much rarer *X. pudens* differs in its velvety-tomentose dark brown cap and brownish stem.

Oudemansiella mucida (Schrader) Hohn

Cap: 5–10cm (2–4in)

Spores: white, 14–18 x 12–16μm, smooth

Edibility: inedible

To see a beech trunk covered in great masses and drifts of the shining white caps of this species is one of the highlights of an autumn walk through the woods. It is one of the most viscid and glutinous of fungi, being covered with a thick layer of clear mucus on both cap and stem. The latter has a distinct white ring near the top and is very tough and fibrous. The broad gills are snow-white and widely spaced. It is reported to produce an antibiotic called mucidin, which is apparently effective against skin fungi.

Marasmius androsaceus (Linnaeus ex Fries)
Fries – 'Horsehair Fungus'
> **Cap:** 0.6–1cm (¼–½in)
> **Spores:** white, 6–9 x 2.5–4.5µm, smooth
> **Edibility:** inedible

The common name of Horsehair Fungus refers to the extremely thin, hair-like, blackish-brown stems of this species which are very long and on which the tiny, elegantly fluted brown caps are uplifted. The gills are very widely spaced and dull flesh-brown. It can be very common, growing in very large numbers on the needle and cone litter of conifer woods throughout Britain. Unlike many species of *Marasmius*, there is no particular odour.

Marasmius rotula (Scopoli ex Fries) Fries
> **Cap:** 0.15–1cm (¹⁄₁₆–½ in)
> **Spores:** white, 6–10 x 3–5µm, smooth
> **Edibility:** inedible

This tiny, pretty mushroom is one of our commonest species of *Marasmius* and can be found dotting the woodland floor on fallen twigs and wood almost anywhere. The bell-shaped cap is white, pleated and sunken at the centre. The white gills are widely spaced, attached to the stem or separated by a narrow collar. The cap has been likened to an open parachute, which is a very good description. The thread-like stem is dark brown and shiny. There is no special odour present.

Marasmius oreades (Bolton) Fries –
'Fairy ring Mushroom'
> **Cap:** 2.5–7.5cm (1–3in)
> **Spores:** white, 7–10 x 4–6µm, smooth
> **Edibility:** edible and excellent

Although many other species of fungi form fairy rings, this is the most well known all over the world since it 'disfigures' lawns and golf courses everywhere. Of course, to mushroom lovers it is a wonderful sight to see the often enormous rings of dark green grass with the mushrooms fruiting on the outer edge. The expansion of the ring can be traced year after year, and some truly gigantic rings many hundreds of metres across are thought to be well over a thousand years old. Indeed, it has even been suggested that some rings may be among the oldest inhabitants of this planet. The tough pale buff caps are smooth, and the gills are thick and widely spaced. The stems are tough and fibrous and are not usually eaten.

Marasmius alliaceus (Jacquin ex Fries) Fries
Cap: 2.5–5cm (1–2in)
Spores: pale cream, 7–11 x 6–8µm, smooth
Edibility: inedible

Another example of a mushroom which is recognizable by its odour, this time with a strong smell of garlic. The bell-shaped, buff cap and tall, thin, stiff, black velvety stem are also distinctive. The habitat is exclusively on fallen beech branches, twigs and so forth. Some other *Marasmius* species also smell of garlic, but they grow in different habitats, for example, *M. scorodonius*, which grows on needle litter in conifer woods and has a smooth, paler stem. See also *Micromphale foetidum*, below.

Micromphale foetidum (Sowerby ex Fries) Singer
Cap: 1–2.5cm (½–1in)
Spores: white, 8.5–10 x 3.5–4µm, smooth
Edibility: inedible

The specific name *foetidum* means stinking or odorous, which is a fitting description of this mushroom as it combines the smell of garlic with overtones of rotted cabbage or fish. The dark red-brown cap is flattened and wrinkled and quite tough. The slender stem is rather short, blackish-brown and velvety. The fungus grows in clumps, often in large numbers, on fallen twigs and branches of beech and hazel. This is in contrast to the single stems of *Marasmius alliaceus* described above.

Collybia maculata (Albertini & Schweinitz ex Fries) Kummer
Cap: 5–10cm (2–4in)
Spores: pale pinkish-buff, 5–6 x 4–5µm, smooth
Edibility: edible but tough

This is sometimes given the common name of cocoa-caps because of the cocoa-coloured spots and stains which soon spread over the initially white cap and gills. The whole mushroom is very tough and sinewy and the cap is very rounded with an incurved margin. The gills are very shallow and crowded. The thick stem can be rather spindle shaped and rooting. It is a common species and can form fairy rings in the litter of the beech or conifer woods in which it likes to grow.

Collybia butyracea (Bulliard ex Fries) Quélet

Cap: 5–7.5cm (2–3in)
Spores: cream-buff, 6–8 x 3–4µm, smooth
Edibility: edible but poor

The name *butyracea* means buttery or greasy and this refers to the texture of the cap surface, which in humid conditions is very slippery and greasy without actually being glutinous or viscid. The cap varies from the dark brown shown to greyish forms referred to as the variety *asema*, and it is hygrophanous. The gills are broad, cream and often rather serrated on the margins. The stem is characteristically tapered upwards from a swollen base. It is a common species, growing in troops across the needle litter under pines and occasionally under deciduous trees too.

Collybia dryophila (Bulliard ex Fries) Kummer

Cap: 2.5–7.5cm (1–3in)
Spores: pale cream, 5–6 x 2–3µm, smooth
Edibility: edible but poor

A contender for the title of commonest mushroom, this species is found all over the temperate regions of the world in a wide variety of habitats. The thin, flattened caps are smooth and dry and vary from reddish-brown to pale yellow-ochre when dry. The crowded gills are thin, narrow and pale cream. The smooth stem is slender and pale orange-brown with white hairs at the base. It grows singly but in groups in both coniferous and deciduous woods, and has a particular preference for oak and pine.

Collybia fusipes (Bulliard ex Fries) Quélet – 'Spindle Shanks'

Cap: 5–10cm (2–4in)
Spores: white, 4–6 x 3–4.5µm, smooth
Edibility: inedible

The fleshy, smooth caps are domed and pale brick-red to reddish-buff but become spotted and stained darker red-brown with age. The thick, broad gills are widely spaced and pale whitish-buff to reddish-brown. The stem, which gives it the common name, is indeed spindle-shaped and is exceedingly tough and fibrous. Its rooting and many stems are loosely joined at the base to form often enormous clumps at the base of oaks. It is a common species in southern England, appearing early in the season; scarcer further north.

Collybia confluens (Persoon ex Fries) Kummer

Cap: 2.5–5cm (1–2in)
Spores: white, 7–10 x 2–4μm, smooth
Edibility: inedible

The densely clustered groups with the hairy, pale brown stems fused together are very distinctive. The top of the stem widens to form a small 'button' which is easily separable from the cap. The rounded, thin caps are grey-brown to pinkish and dry, while the gills are narrow, very crowded and cream. There is a curious aromatic odour which is quite pleasant. It is a common species and grows in fallen leaf or needle litter in mixed woods throughout Britain.

Mycena galopus (Persoon ex Fries) Kummer

Cap: 0.6–1cm (¼–½ in)
Spores: white, 10–14 x 5–7μm, smooth
Edibility: inedible

This is one of a series of species which exudes a 'milk' or latex when broken and quite fresh. In this species the milk is white, while in others it may be red or orange. The tiny bell-shaped cap is grey-brown to beige, fading with age. The gills are pale greyish-white and the stem is grey-brown to reddish-brown with a hairy base. When snapped the hollow stem drips white latex. It is very common growing singly, scattered over the leaf litter of coniferous and mixed woods everywhere. *M. leucogala* is dark grey-black, but otherwise similar, except for some minor microscopic differences. It is sometimes referred to as a variety (*nigra*) of the species described here.

Mycena galericulata (Scopoli ex Fries) S. F. Gray

Cap: 2.5–5cm (1–2in)
Spores: white, 8–11 x 5.5–7μm, smooth
Edibility: edible but poor

This very common species is quite variable in colour, size and shape and causes most beginners a lot of difficulty in recognition. The features to look for are the rather bluntly conical cap, which is dull grey-brown and radially wrinkled. The gills are white to greyish or even pinkish when mature, and are noticeably interveined with cross-veins. The smooth stem is shiny, greyish, fused into clumps and often deeply rooting into the wood on which it grows.

Mycena inclinata (Fries) Quélet

Cap: 2.5–5cm (1–2in)
Spores: white, 8–10 x 5.5–7μm, smooth
Edibility: edibility doubtful, best avoided

Often confused with the previous species and vice versa, this species has a grey-brown, bell-shaped cap which is minutely but distinctly toothed along the margin. The gills are grey-white to pinkish. The stem is smooth, becoming strongly reddish-brown to orange-brown in the lower half, and the surface is flecked with minute tufts of white cottony hairs (use a hand-lens for this). There is a distinct odour, difficult to define but suggestive of cheap soap or even cucumber. It grows in small tufts on fallen logs and stumps, especially oaks, everywhere.

Mycena haematopus (Persoon ex Fries) Kummer

Cap: 1–5cm (½–2in)
Spores: white, 9–10 x 6.5–7μm, smooth
Edibility: inedible

Sometimes called the Bleeding Mycena, this name refers to the dark reddish-brown juice which 'bleeds' from the stem when broken. The small, bell-shaped caps are dark reddish-brown to wine-red and have small teeth along the margin. The stems are slender, smooth and coloured like the cap. This species is usually found in clusters on fallen timber and is a common species throughout Britain. The juice will stain the fingers for some time.

Mycena pura (Persoon ex Fries) Kummer

Cap: 2.5–5cm (1–2in)
Spores: white, 5–9 x 3–4μm, smooth
Edibility: inedible; has been suspected of causing poisoning

A common odour in many mushrooms is that of radish – referred to as raphanoid – and nowhere is this better demonstrated than in this species which both smells and tastes of radishes. The rather robust cap and stem are a delicate lilac-pink to purplish-grey, or even blue-grey. Although the colours seem to vary considerably, depending on the habitat, the smell nevertheless remains constant. It is a common species in both deciduous and coniferous woodlands throughout Britain. The rarer *M. pelianthina* described below has dark purplish gill edges, while *M. rosea* has a more bell-shaped cap without an umbo. *M. diosma* has a strong odour of tobacco and constantly grey or brown-violet gills.

Mycena polygramma (Bulliard ex Fries) S. F. Gray

Cap: 2.5–5cm (1–2in)
Spores: white, 8–10 x 5.5–7µm, smooth
Edibility: inedible

A hand-lens is useful to identify this species because you need to look very closely at the stem, where very fine silvery lines may be seen running lengthwise in young fruit-bodies. The cap is bell-shaped to domed and a dark blue-grey to grey-brown. The narrow gills are pale greyish-white. It grows in small tufts on fallen deciduous wood and is quite common.

Mycena pelianthina (Fries) Quélet

Cap: 2.5–5cm (1–2in)
Spores: white, 4.5–6 x 2.5–3µm, smooth
Edibility: inedible

Often confused with *Mycena pura* described above, this species has rather similar pinkish-lilac to grey-lilac or violet-brown colours, but has a distinctly transparently lined cap margin and the gill edges are also dark violet-brown. The stem is thick, smooth and coloured like the cap. The whole mushroom has a strong odour of radishes, especially when rubbed. It is fairly common and grows in small groups on fallen beech leaves.

Mycena sanguinolenta (Albertini & Schweinitz ex Fries) Kummer

Cap: 0.6–1cm (¼–½ in)
Spores: white, 8–11 x 4–6µm, smooth
Edibility: inedible

This very delicate, slender species is another of those mushrooms which 'bleed' when broken, this time a reddish juice from the stem. The small, bell-shaped cap is reddish-brown to purplish-brown, while the gills are whitish. The slender stem is pale reddish-brown. Unlike *M. haematopus*, which also bleeds when cut, it grows singly in small troops on decaying leaf or needle litter and is widespread throughout Britain.

Mycena epipterygia (Scopoli) S. F. Gray

Cap: 0.6–1cm (¼–½ in)
Spores: white, 8–12 x 4–6µm, smooth
Edibility: inedible

A few species of *Mycena*, as in this case, are very sticky, especially when wet. In this species both the cap and stem are sticky and are coloured a pale greenish-yellow, becoming greyer with age. The gills are white to lemon. It is a common species and occurs in mossy areas under conifers and under bracken on heaths and moors, as well as on dead conifer wood. It is an amazingly variable species with numerous described varieties which might at first be considered species, except that they all seem to intergrade one into another. The slightly darker, greener and stouter *M. epipterygioides* is found on dead conifer stumps.

AMANITACEAE
Amanita family

There are over 20 species of *Amanita* in Britain and the genus contains some of the most beautiful, and the most deadly, mushrooms in the world. Features to look for are the white, smooth spores, and the universal veil, which may be left as a sac-like volva at the stem base or as mere warty remnants on the cap and stem base. A partial veil may also be present as a skirt-like ring or annulus at the top of the stem. Always make sure to collect the entire stem base from under the ground so any volva can be seen. Some *Amanita* species have distinctive odours. The gills are free from the stem, as seen in the cross-section below.

A second genus usually included in this family is *Limacella*, which has a slimy veil.

Amanita phalloides (Fries) Saccardo –
'Death Cap'
  Cap: 5–15cm (2–6in)
  Spores: white, 8–10.5 x 7–8μm, amyloid
  Edibility: deadly poisonous; kills many people
  every year in Europe

This species has been accidentally introduced from Europe to North America, where it is spreading rapidly. It contains complex chemicals called amatoxins and phallotoxins which can cause severe liver damage, preceded by painful and intensive vomiting and diarrhoea, muscle cramps and general debilitation. Unfortunately, the symptoms rarely appear until several hours after the mushroom is eaten, making prompt recognition and treatment difficult. The yellowish-green to olive cap may also be brownish or even completely white in some forms. The ring and large, bulbous volva are distinctive, as is the sweet, sickly odour which develops with age – rather like old honey. In its white form it may be mistaken for a Horse Mushroom (*Agaricus* species), but unlike that genus the gills and spores are pure white. It grows from late summer onwards, especially in the south under oaks and occasionally conifers.

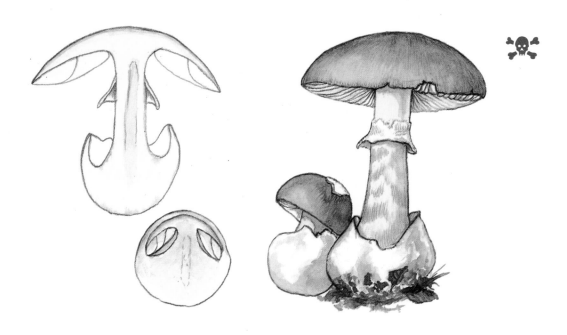

Amanita virosa Secretan –
'Destroying Angel'
>**Cap**: 5–15cm (2–6in)
>**Spores**: 9–11 x 7–9µm, amyloid
>**Edibility**: deadly poisonous; contains similar toxins
>to the Death Cap, (page 83)

As beautiful as it is deadly, this species well deserves its common name. All parts of the mushroom are pure white and the cap is frequently slightly sticky and rather bluntly rounded to almost conical. The slender stem is slightly woolly-scaly and has a large volval sac at the base. The odour is faint, sickly sweet of honey. A good test for this species is to place a drop of caustic soda (KOH) on the cap, which will turn bright golden-yellow. Fortunately, this is a rare species in Britain, being most common in the Scottish Highlands. Compare it carefully with *A. citrina* var. *alba* (see p.86).

Amanita submembranacea Bon
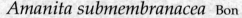
>**Cap**: 7.5–10cm (3–4in)
>**Spores**: white, 9–12µm, rounded and non-amyloid
>**Edibility**: uncertain; best avoided, like all *Amanita* species

Often misidentified, this may prove to be more common than is thought at present. The dark grey-brown to olive-brown cap can be quite dark and has long striations at the margin; there are often flakes of universal veil clinging to the cap surface. The tall stem is banded with faint yellow-brown to grey-brown zones and there is a thick, grey-white volva at the base. There is no ring or annulus present on the stem. Although it has been recorded from a number of localities in Britain, it appears to be commonest in Scotland.

Amanita vaginata (Bulliard ex Fries) Vittadini
>**Cap**: 5–10cm (2–4in)
>**Spores**: white, 9–12µm, globose, non-amyloid
>**Edibility**: edible but best avoided

This elegant species is another of the 'ringless' *Amanita* species, sometimes called *Amanitopsis* in older literature. The cap is a pale grey to steel-grey with a deeply grooved margin while the gills are white. The slender stem is pale grey with faint, darker bands and has a white volva at the base. Found in mixed woods throughout Britain, it appears to be commoner in the north.

Amanita fulva (Schaeffer ex Fries) Persoon – 'Tawny Grisette'

Cap: 5–10cm (2–4in)
Spores: white, 8–10μm, globose, non-amyloid
Edibility: edible but best avoided

One of the commonest species in Britain, it can be found in almost any woodland and is quite variable in colour. Usually it is a rich orange-brown to reddish-brown but may be paler or darker. The gills are crowded, cream and often have minutely jagged edges. The stem is cream with faint brownish bands and has a white volval sac with the inner surface pale brown. There is no ring present on the stem. The common name of Tawny Grisette is of European origin (probably French).

Amanita ceciliae (Berkeley & Broom) Bas
[= *A. inaurata*]

Cap: 5–12.5cm (2–5in)
Spores: white, 11.5–14μm, globose, non-amyloid
Edibility: edibility uncertain, best avoided

A large and rather rare species, the cap is dark grey-brown, smooth and usually has fragments of greyish veil left on the surface as warts. The gills are greyish-white and crowded. The tall, rather stout stem is pale greyish with darker bands of woolly grey. At the base the volval remnants form broken, constricted fragments and these are often left behind in the soil when it is picked. There is no ring present on the upper stem. It grows in mixed woods throughout Britain and until recently has been more widely known under the synonym *A. inaurata*.

Amanita battarae (Boudier) Bon
[= *A. umbrinolutea*]

Cap: 7.5–12.5cm (3–5in)
Spores: white, 11–16 x 9.5–13μm, non-amyloid
Edibility: doubtful and best avoided

A rare but very striking species, often of great stature. The cap is curiously zoned with a darker band behind the marginal grooves, and is coloured in shades of olive-brown to yellow-brown. The gills are broad, free of the stem and cream. The stout stem is buff with darker, slightly woolly bands and emerges from a thick and very prominent white or pale buff volva. It has been found in southern England in coniferous woods and also under beech. It is probably edible like others in the ringless group of *Amanita* but is best avoided to prevent any confusion with the more dangerous species.

Amanita crocea (Quélet) Singer

Cap: 7.5–12.5 (3–5in)
Spores: white, 8–12μm, rounded, non-amyloid
Edibility: doubtful; best avoided

Perhaps the loveliest of the ringless *Amanita* species, with its cap and stem a clear, bright orange-buff to orange-brown and the gills a pale orange-cream. The stem is strikingly banded with orange-buff woolly scales and emerges from a thick cream-white volva, which usually has a pale orange inner surface. Its distribution is rather unusual, being commonest in Scotland, but with large fruitings having been seen in southern England too.

Amanita citrina var. alba (Gillet) Gilbert

Cap: 7.5–12.5cm (3–5in)
Spores: white, 7–10μm, rounded, amyloid
Edibility: inedible

A beautiful species sometimes mistaken for the Destroying Angel (*A. virosa*), but differing from that species in a number of features. The white, rounded cap usually has numerous fragments of veil adhering to it and the smooth stem has a very large rounded bulb with a gutter-like upper margin (not the bag-like volva of *A. virosa*). The gills and flesh have a strong odour of freshly dug potatoes. There is a well-developed ring at the top of the stem. A common species found under beech throughout Britain. Although this is usually considered a variety of *A. citrina* (see below), it might be regarded as a species in its own right. It is consistently larger and more robust, does not intergrade in its features and is more restricted in its habitat.

Amanita citrina Schaeffer ex S. F. Gray

Cap: 5–10cm (2–4in)
Spores: white, 7–10μm, rounded, amyloid
Edibility: inedible

The lovely pale lemon-yellow cap is frequently patterned with patches of whitish veil, while the stem and ring are also tinted pale yellow. The stem has a large rounded bulb with a gutter-like upper margin. A strong odour of freshly dug potatoes is present in the gills and flesh and helps distinguish it from the similar (*A. phalloides*). A very common species throughout Britain, it grows in mixed woods, both deciduous and coniferous.

Amanita porphyria (Albertini & Schweinitz ex Fries) Secretan

Cap: 2.5–7.5cm (1–3in)
Spores: white, 7–9μm, globose, amyloid
Edibility: inedible, possibly poisonous

A close relative of the previous species and rather similar in its shape and particularly in its bulbous base. Its coloration, however, is very different, being grey-brown with distinct hints of lilac, especially in the ring and stem. The odour is weaker than in *A. citrina* and may be of potato or radish. This is a rather uncommon species in Britain and grows in both coniferous and deciduous woods.

Amanita eliae Quélet

Cap: 5–10cm (2–4in)
Spores: white, 11–14 x 6.5–8.5μm, non-amyloid
Edibility: uncertain, best avoided

One of our rarest species in this genus, it is also unusual in having a ring but no obvious volva at the stem base. The colours are pale pinkish-ochre to buff and the cap has fine marginal grooves. The stem may be quite deeply rooted into the soil and has a white, very fragile ring. It appears to like sandy or acid soils and is widespread in Britain.

Amanita muscaria (Linnaeus ex Fries) Hooker – 'Fly Agaric'

Cap: 7.5–25cm (3–10in)
Spores: white, 9.5–13 x 6.5–8.5μm, non-amyloid
Edibility: poisonous, although rarely deadly

There can be few people who do not recognize the traditional fairy-tale mushroom with the red cap and white spots, although many are surprised to find that it really exists outside children's books. The large, scarlet-red cap is smooth and slightly sticky at first, enclosed in a white or yellowish veil which breaks up into warty fragments. The stem is bulbous, with bands of warty veil around the top of the bulb, and there is a large, floppy ring hanging down. The common name refers to its use in country districts as a remedy against houseflies.The skin of the cap is peeled off and placed in a saucer of milk which both attracts and then poisons the flies. It is a common species often found in rings in birch and occasionally pine woods throughout Britain.

Amanita pantherina (A. P. de Candolle ex Fries) Secretan – 'Panther Cap'

Cap: 5–10cm (2–4in)

Spores: white, 8–14 x 6.5–10μm, non-amyloid

Edibility: poisonous and dangerous

The pale grey-brown to dark brown cap is strikingly spotted with pure white warty fragments of veil. The gills, stem and ring are all white. The stem has a round bulb with a gutter-like margin and usually with one or more narrow rings of white veil immediately above it. This species is distinctly uncommon in Britain and grows in mixed woods, especially in the south. It is a very poisonous species, causing delirium, vomiting and finally a coma-like sleep. On rare occasions it even causes death.

Amanita friabilis Karsten

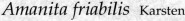

Cap: 2.5–7.5cm (1–3in)

Spores: white, 9.5–14 x 7–10.5μm, non-amyloid

Edibility: edibility unknown; best avoided

Some mushrooms are extremely specific in their choice of habitat and if it happens to be an unusual one, they may be overlooked. This may well be the case here. *A. friabilis* grows only in stands of alder trees (*Alnus*), and since these are usually boggy and difficult areas to move through, they are often neglected. So, although it is assumed that this species is rare, it may be commoner than supposed. It is a small species with a woolly, grey-brown cap and stem and without a volva.

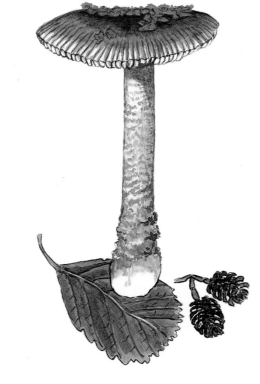

Amanita gemmata (Fries) Gillet

[=A. junquillea]

Cap: 5–10cm (2–4in)

Spores: white, 8.5–11 x 5.5–8.5μm, non-amyloid

Edibility: possibly poisonous

Rather uncommon in Britain, it is one of a group of species, including the dangerous *A. pantherin*a, which have a rounded bulb with a gutter-like upper margin. The extent of the toxicity of this species is uncertain and debated. There may be localized varieties which are more poisonous than others, or perhaps it is a complex of species which remains to be sorted out and distinguished. Certainly there seem to be cases of quite severe poisoning on record, particularly in Europe and North America, where this species also occurs. It is distinguished by its pale butter-yellow to ochre cap with white veil patches and fragile ring on the stem.

Amanita rubescens (Persoon ex Fries)
S. F. Gray – 'Blusher'
    Cap: 5–15cm (2–6in)
    Spores: white, 8–10 x 5-6µm, amyloid
    Edibility: edible but best avoided

This very common fungus has the common name of Blusher, which refers to the flush of pinkish-red which appears in the flesh, especially at the stem base, either when injured or with age. All parts of the mushroom will eventually become a dull reddish colour, and this can make it difficult for the unpractised eye to recognize. When young the cap may be almost white, pale yellowish-brown to almost pink, usually with numerous small groups of whitish veil remnants like warts. The stem base is rounded but without a veil, and there is a well-formed ring above. It grows in almost any woodland throughout Britain.

Amanita rubescens var. *annulosulphurea* Gillet
    Cap: 5–7.5cm (2–3in)
    Spores: white, 8–10 x 5–6µm, amyloid
    Edibility: edible but best avoided

Variations of colour or form do not usually get a formal name unless particularly striking or, as in this instance, very consistent. This variant is usually rather smaller in size and has a bright sulphur-yellow ring. Because of its constancy it is sometimes regarded as a species in its own right by some authorities. It is rather uncommon and grows in deciduous woods throughout Britain.

Amanita spissa (Fries) Kummer [= *A. excelsa*?]
    Cap: 5–15cm (2–6in)
    Spores: white, 9–10 x 7–8µm, amyloid
    Edibility: probably edible but best avoided

A very common and very variable species, usually rather squat and robust with grey-brown colours and a bulbous, rooting stem which is grey woolly-scaly and has a white ring. A distinctive odour of potato or radish is present. Several variants have been given names, in particular a large pearly grey form with a long, slender, deeply rooting stem and a pleasant fruity odour; this is often regarded as a separate species, *A. excelsa*. Other authorities regard it as just a variety. *A. spissa* grows in mixed woods throughout Britain.

Amanita franchetii (Boudier) Fayod

[=A. aspera]

Cap: 5–15cm (2–6in)

Spores: white, 8–10 x 6–7μm, amyloid

Edibility: edibility uncertain; best avoided

An unusual species, quite attractive, being essentially a dark brown-capped species with bright yellow veil remnants on the cap, ring edge and upper edge of the stem bulb. The flesh is white and hardly discolours, unlike that of *A. rubescens* which it may perhaps resemble. It seems to be rather rare almost everywhere but is perhaps commonest in woodlands in southern England.

Amanita strobiliformis (Vittadini) Quélet

[=A. solitaria]

Cap: 10–25cm (4–10in)

Spores: white, 9–14 x 7–9.5μm, amyloid

Edibility: apparently edible but to be avoided

One of the largest and most striking mushrooms to be found anywhere, the young buttons of this species may be larger than the adults of most other species. The entire fungus is pure white and covered with a thick covering of soft, woolly warts or scales. The stem is tall and rooting with a woolly surface and a very soft, ragged ring which has the consistency of cream cheese. The cap margin is usually festooned with ragged veil remnants. It is a locally common species in southern England and prefers chalky soils under beech trees. The very rare A. *vittadinii* differs in its slender, spindle-shaped, pointed stem, which is scaly up to the ring, small flattened cap scales and generally smaller stature. It is found in southern England on calcareous soils.

Amanita echinocephala (Vittadini) Quélet

Cap: 7.5–12.5cm (3–5in)

Spores: greenish-white, 9.5–11 x 6.5–7.5μm, amyloid

Edibility: inedible

Closely related to the previous species, it is rarer and easily distinguished by its small, sharply pointed pyramidal warts on the cap, and the stem which is narrowly pointed and banded with scaly zones. The gills and spores have an unusual faint greenish-white tint and the flesh has an odd odour reminiscent of old ham or perhaps alkali. Like *A. strobiliformis,* it prefers chalky soils under beech and is commonest in southern England.

Chamaemyces fracidus (Fries) Donk

[=*Drosella fracida*]

Cap: 2.5–7.5cm (1–3in)

Spores: pale buff, 4.5–5 x 2–2.5μm

Edibility: inedible

A species which has changed its name more than once and whose relationship to other mushrooms is uncertain, but which is often placed here, next to *Amanita* or in the next family, the *Lepiotaceae*. It is an odd species with a pale ivory-buff cap which is slightly wrinkled and usually marked with reddish-brown patches. The white gills are free and often weep droplets of dark liquid. The stem is whitish with a woolly surface up to a faint ring-zone. The flesh has a peculiar odour of rubber or tar. It grows in grass at woodland edges, especially under young conifers in southern England.

Limacella glioderma (Fries) Maire

Cap: 2.5–7.5cm (1–3in)

Spores: white, 3–4μm, globose, non–amyloid

Edibility: edibility unknown; best avoided

An extremely glutinous, slippery species, it nevertheless seems to be closely related to the drier members of the genus *Amanita* or perhaps *Lepiota.* The cap is dark reddish-brown to pinkish and often granular under the slime. The gills (as in *Amanita*) are white and free from the stem. The stem is light brown and slimy, and the flesh has a strong odour of new meal. This, and the few other species that make up the genus *Limacella,* are all rather rare. In this instance it grows under birch and hemlock and is widespread in Britain.

LEPIOTACEAE
Lepiota family

A large family of mushrooms ranging from tiny, delicate species to some of the largest mushrooms in the world. A number are considered good edibles, while others are dangerously poisonous and are known to contain similar toxins to those found in the infamous and deadly *Amanita* mushrooms. The family is characterized by free gills, white to pale pinkish-cream or green spores and usually a more or less obvious ring on the stem. They are related to the black-brown spored *Agaricus* mushrooms.

Lepiota ignivolvata Bousser-Josserand
Cap: 7.5–12.5cm (3–5in)
Spores: white, 11–13 x 5–6μm, spindle shaped
Edibility: unknown

This is a rare species, and among other whitish-buff species is best distinguished by the narrow reddish-brown rings at the stem base, the odour of rubber and the flesh which slowly flushes red in the stem base. The cap surface is finely scaly with a brown central umbo. It grows on chalky soils under conifers. Like many species, the edibility is unrecorded and, in view of the deadly nature of some of the smaller species, is best avoided.

Lepiota felina (Persoon) Karsten
Cap: 2.5–4cm (1–1½in)
Spores: white, 6.5–7.5 x 3.5–4μm, oval
Edibility: unknown, possibly poisonous

There are numerous small, delicate species of Lepiota and they are distinguished by cap colour and scaliness, odours, staining and spore shape. In this instance the spores are oval; other species have bullet-shaped or spindle-shaped spores. The cap is white with tiny black scales and there is a thin, black-edged ring on the stem. There is usually an odour of cedarwood present. It is uncommon but widely distributed in coniferous woods.

Lepiota ventriosospora Reid
Cap: 5–7.5cm (2–3in)
Spores: white, 14–18 x 4–6μm, spindle-shaped
Edibility: unknown, best avoided

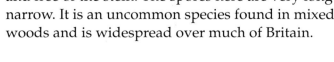

A medium-sized species with a yellow-ochre to yellow-brown scaly cap, brighter at the margin and with a slender woolly stem, also yellowish. The gills are white and free of the stem. The spores here are very long and narrow. It is an uncommon species found in mixed woods and is widespread over much of Britain.

Lepiota castanea Quélet

Cap: 2.5–5cm (1–2in)
Spores: white, 9–13 x 3.5–5µm, bullet shaped
with the apiculus offset
Edibility: inedible, probably poisonous

This species may be recognized by the overall
chestnut-brown scales which cover the cap and the
lower half of the stem. The gills are free, white and
sometimes have small rust-brown spots. The spores
are distinctively bullet shaped. This is one of our
commoner species and can be found in mixed
woods, especially in the south of England.

Lepiota brunneoincarnata Chodoir & Mart

Cap: 2.5–5cm (1–2in)
Spores: white, 7–9 x 4–5µm, oval
Edibility: extremely poisonous, even deadly

It is only in recent years that it has become clear that
other groups beside *Amanita* can contain deadly toxins,
and the genus *Lepiota* is now known to have several
species with the same complex phalloidin chemicals,
which can kill if eaten. Most of the species concerned
are small, often with brownish-purplish colours and
scaly caps. However, many others are simply untested
and all small *Lepiota* species must be avoided as far as
eating is concerned. This species is rather stocky, with a
fairly short, stout stem and purple-brown scales on the
cap and lower stem, and often with an overall wine-
pink flush. It can be fairly frequent in grassy clearings,
woodland edges and hedgerows, and even gardens.

Lepiota cristata (Fries) Kummer –
'Stinking Lepiota'

Cap: 1–5cm (½–2in)
Spores: white, 5–7 x 3–4µm, bullet shaped with
the apiculus offset
Edibility: possibly poisonous

The common name refers to the strong, unpleasant odour
of rubber, or of the common Earthball (*Scleroderma*), which
is present in the gills and flesh. This is probably our
commonest small *Lepiota* species and is recognized by the
white cap marked with dark reddish-brown scales, and
the white stem which is smooth and has a tiny white ring
near the top. It can be found in grassy areas in mixed
woods, on roadsides and in gardens everywhere.

Lepiota clypeolaria (Bulliard ex Fries) Kummer

Cap: 2.5–7.5cm (1–3in)
Spores: white, 12–16 x 4–5µm, spindle shaped
Edibility: inedible, possibly poisonous

A rather attractive, woolly-scaly species. The specific name means 'shield-like', which is a good description of the cap with its pale brown, scaly surface and darker, smooth central umbo. The stem is distinctive as it is clothed in woolly-shaggy scales up to an apical ring-zone. The flesh is nearly odourless. It grows in mixed woods, especially under conifers, and is widespread in Britain, although commonest in the south.

Cystolepiota aspera (Persoon)

Bon [=*Lepiota aspera*]
Cap: 5–15cm (2–6in)
Spores: white, 6–8 x 2.5–4µm, almost fusiform
Edibility: inedible, possibly poisonous

The genus *Cystolepiota* is separated from *Lepiota* by the cap cuticle, which is composed of numerous globose cells forming a powdery or warty surface. In this large species the warts are quite small and sharply pointed. The cap tends to be almost bluntly conical and is chestnut to pale brown. The gills are white and repeatedly forked and very crowded. The stout stem is pale brown with similar small scales up to a well-formed floppy ring. The flesh has a strong odour of rubber or of the common Earthball (*Scleroderma*). Quite common, it grows under beech.

Cystolepiota bucknallii (Berkeley & Broom)

Singer & Clemençon [=*Lepiota bucknallii*]
Cap: 1–2.5cm (½–1in)
Spores: white, 7–8 x 3–4µm, elliptic
Edibility: unknown, possibly poisonous

Easily identified, this species is unique in having a lavender flush at the base of the stem combined with a strong odour of coal gas. The remainder of this small mushroom is white and the cap surface is powdery. The gills are a pale ochre and rather widely spaced. It can be quite common in shady woods and thickets on rich soils under deciduous trees. The small *C. seminuda* is also white with a faint lavender stem base, but is odourless and has white gills.

Cystolepiota seminuda (Lasch) Bon

Cap: 1cm (½in)
Spores: white, 3.5–4 x 2.5–3µm, elliptic
Edibility: unknown, possibly poisonous

One of the smallest and most delicate species, the white cap has a powdery surface. The free gills are white, rather crowded. The slender stem is white and flushed lilac-grey below. Unlike the similar but larger *C. bucknallii*, there is no particular odour present. It is a common species, but often overlooked because of its small size, and grows on rich, shady soils along paths and tracks, hedgerows and thickets.

Melanophyllum haematospermum
(Bulliard) Kreisel [=*Lepiota echinata*]

Cap: 2.5–5cm (1–2in)

Spores: greenish but soon drying dull reddish,
5–6 x 3–3.5µm, elliptic to almost kidney-shaped

Edibility: inedible

A strange species separated from *Lepiota* because of
its coloured spore print and coloured gills. In this
species the cap and stem are dark yellow-brown to
grey-brown and slightly granular-powdery. The
gills are dark wine-reddish. It is an uncommon
species, although probably often overlooked. It
grows on rich soils in nettle beds, disturbed areas,
under shrubs in woods and gardens.

Melanophyllum eyrei (Massee) Singer
[=*Lepiota eyrei*]

Cap: 1–2.5cm (½–1in)

Spores: pale green, 3.5–4 x 2.5µm, elliptic

Edibility: inedible

Unique in the strange colour of the gills, which are a
clear blue-green. The cap and stem are whitish to
cream-ochre and finely powdery-granular; the cap
margin is usually hung with traces of veil. This
small species is quite uncommon but can be found
on rich, damp soils below beech, ash and oak trees,
often under low herbaceous plants. It is mostly
found in southern England.

Leucocoprinus birnbaumi (Corda) Singer
[=*Lepiota lutea*]

Cap: 1–2.5cm (½–1in)

Spores: white, 8–13 x 5–8µm, smooth

Edibility: unknown

Leucocoprinus species share the common features of
a fragile, usually small body with a strongly
striated-pleated cap margin and spores with a
germ-pore at the end. This species is known from all
over the world, but is almost certainly an
introduction from some tropical region since in cool
countries such as Britain it occurs only in
glasshouses or in homes in potted plants. The
brilliant yellow coloration of all its parts, finely
granular-scaly surface and extreme fragility are all
unmistakable.

Macrolepiota procera (Scopoli) Singer –

'Parasol Mushroom' [=*Lepiota procera*]

> **Cap**: 10–25cm (4–10in)
> **Spores**: white to cream, 15–20 x 10–13µm, elliptical
> **Edibility**: edible and delicious

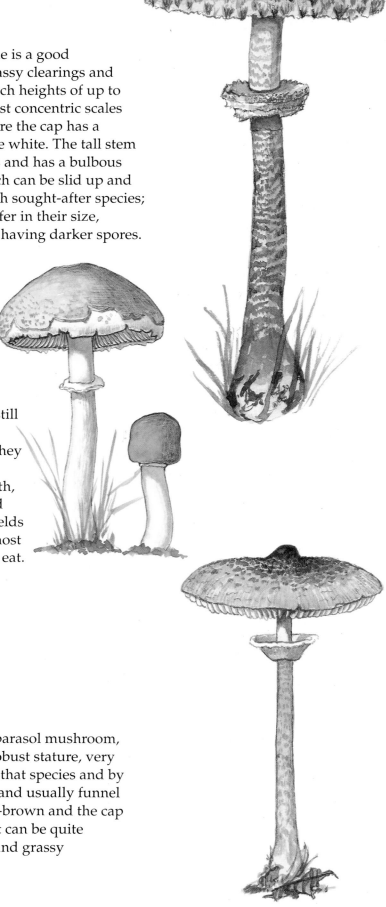

One of our most magnificent species, the common name is a good description of its general appearance, as it stands in grassy clearings and fields and looks very much like a tall parasol. It can reach heights of up to 45cm (18in). The cap is whitish-brown with thick, almost concentric scales formed by the break-up of the outer cuticle. At the centre the cap has a darker brown blunt umbo. The broad, crowded gills are white. The tall stem is very stiff and cross-banded with darker brown zones and has a bulbous base. There is a thick, whitish double-layered ring which can be slid up and down the stem when loose. This is a delicious and much sought-after species; one cap can fill a frying pan. Closely related species differ in their size, scaliness and lack of banding on the stem, as well as in having darker spores.

Macrolepiota excoriata (Fries) Wasser

[=*Lepiota excoriata*]

> **Cap**: 7.5–12.5cm (3–5in)
> **Spores**: white, 12–15 x 8–9µm, elliptical
> **Edibility**: edible and good

Not as common or as large as the giant parasol, this is still an attractive and interesting species. The cap scales are felty-shaggy, pale cream to milky coffee colour and as they break up they pull back from the margin, exposing the paler flesh below. The stem is white, more or less smooth, without cross-bands, and there is a thin, double-layered ring present. It often grows in large numbers in open fields and pastures and is commonest in the south. As with most of the large parasol mushrooms, this one is delicious to eat.

Macrolepiota gracilenta (Fries) Wasser

[=*Lepiota gracilenta*]

> **Cap**: 7.5–10cm (3–4in)
> **Spores**: cream, 10–13 x 7–8µm, elliptical
> **Edibility**: edible and good

This slender, graceful species is often mistaken for the parasol mushroom, *M. procera*, but may be distinguished by its much less robust stature, very finely scaly stem without the prominent cross-bands of that species and by the smaller spores. The ring on the stem is also thinner and usually funnel shaped when young. Its colours are pale brown to grey-brown and the cap scales are small and pulled back from the cap margin. It can be quite common and seems to grow more often in woodlands and grassy clearings than in open pastures, unlike *M. procera*.

Macrolepiota rhacodes (Vittadini) Singer
[=*Lepiota rhacodes*]
>   **Cap**: 7.5–15cm (3–6in)
>   **Spores**: white, 6–10 x 5–7µm, elliptical
>   **Edibility**: edible and good

This species comes in two varieties, which are sometimes regarded as two species. Illustrated here is the typical variety to be found in woodlands on deep leaf litter or needle beds in conifer woods. It has a dull or dirty brown cap which is finely to coarsely scaly, and a whitish, bulbous stem with a prominent two layered-ring. The flesh bruises reddish-brown. A much larger, more robust variety is more often found in gardens on compost heaps and leaf beds and this has an almost white and very coarsely scaly cap, brown at the centre and with an extremely bulbous stem. This is referred to as the variety *hortensis* but is often considered a species, *L. bohemica*.

Macrolepiota konradii (Huijsman ex Orton)
Moser [=*Lepiota konradii*]
>   **Cap**: 7.5–10cm (3–4in)
>   **Spores**: cream, 11–15 x 8.5–9.5µm, elliptical
>   **Edibility**: edible and excellent

For a long time confused with *M. procera*, it differs in its smaller stature, the cap with the cuticle broken up at the margin in a star-like manner exposing the white flesh beneath, and the stem which is whitish, and smooth with hardly any banding. The spores are also smaller. It favours similar habitats, however, and can be found quite commonly in fields and pastures and along woodland edges.

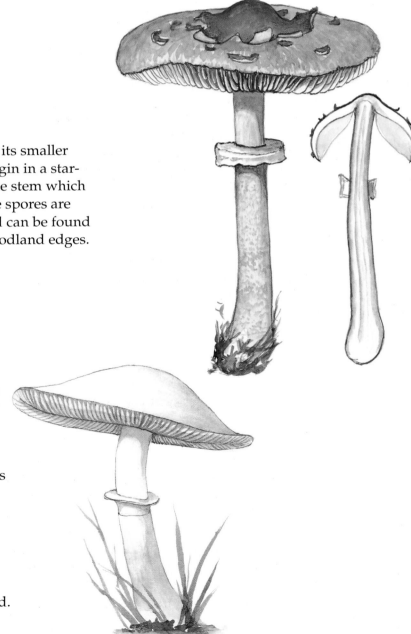

Leucoagaricus leucothites (Vittadini)
Wasser [= *Lepiota naucina*]
>   **Cap**: 5–10cm (2–4in)
>   **Spores**: at first white but later deposits pink
>   **Edibility**: best avoided; has caused some upsets

This all-white species is often mistaken for a field mushroom (*Agaricus*), especially since the gills are pinkish when mature, but careful examination will show that the gills never darken to blackish-brown as in *Agaricus*. This species exhibits an unusual phenomenon in that if a series of spore deposits are taken from a single cap over a period of time, each print will be darker and pinker than the preceding one. The cap and stem discolour to dull grey-brown with handling or ageing. It can be quite common in open fields and woodland edges in southern England.

GOMPHIDIACEAE
Gomphidius Family

These mushrooms actually appear closer to the boletes rather than to other gilled mushrooms because of their very similar spores, body chemistry and other microscopic characters. For convenience however, they are grouped here with other gilled mushrooms. Most species have a veil which may be dry or glutinous.

Two genera occur in Britain, *Chroogomphus* and *Gomphidius*, separated by their reactions to the chemical Melzer's Iodine. In the first genus the flesh is usually a shade of orange, and turns a deep blue-black with the iodine solution. In the second genus the flesh is usually whitish and does not turn blue-black.

Gomphidius roseus (Fries) Karsten
Cap: 2.5–5cm (1–2in)
Spores: almost black, 15–17 x 5–5.5μm, spindle shaped
Edibility: edible but poor

This can be an extraordinarily beautiful species with its bright coral-pink, glutinous cap shining out against the dark needle litter in which it grows. The thick, widely spaced gills are whitish-grey and deeply decurrent. The stem is white, tapered below, with a glutinous veil up to a faint ring-zone.The thick flesh is white and slightly reddish below. This unmistakable species appears to have an odd association with a bolete – *Suillus bovinus* – and wherever one is found the other is also often found in close attendance. It is not known exactly why this happens, but it seems the fruiting of one is stimulated by the other. *G. roseus* is not common, unfortunately, but grows under pines and is widespread in Britain.

Gomphidius glutinosus (Schaeffer ex Fries) Fries

Cap: 5–10cm (2–4in)

Spores: black, 15–21 x 4–7.5μm, spindle shaped

Edibility: edible

Another very slimy species but nevertheless very attractive. The top-shaped cap is a pale greyish-brown to pinkish or purplish-brown with decurrent, thick grey-white gills. The stem is white with a glutinous ring-zone and is bright yellow at the base both within and without. It grows under conifers, especially spruce, and is rather uncommon in Britain. Unlike the previous species, *G. roseus*, there appears to be no particular association with any species of bolete. A related species, *G. maculatus*, is associated with larch trees, and differs in soon spotting rust-brown to black, especially on the stem, its generally more slender stature, and the lack of bright-yellow colour at the base.

Chroogomphus rutilus (Schaeffer ex Fries) Miller [=*Gomphidius rutilus*]

Cap: 5–15cm (2–6in)

Spores: blackish, 15–22 x 5.5–7μm, spindle shaped

Edibility: edible

The genus *Chroogomphus* is separated from *Gomphidius* by its ochrous colours of gills and flesh and by the reaction of many of the fruit-bodies' cells to Melzer's iodine, becoming a deep blue-black. The often large cap of this species is frequently sharply umbonate and is viscid when wet but it soon dries and is orange-brown to copper-reddish. The decurrent gills are ochre then purplish-grey when mature. The stout stem is ochre-orange flushed pale wine-red above and has faint woolly zones below a ring-zone. The solid flesh is ochre-orange. This is a common species and grows under pines throughout Britain. A very rare species, doubtfully recorded from Britain, is *C. helveticus*, which differs in its dry, tomentose-scaly cap.

AGARICACEAE
Agaricus Family

Agaricus provides us with the well-known white mushroom we purchase in greengrocers, as well as the popular Field Mushroom and Horse Mushroom. All species have deep blackish-brown to chocolate spores, free gills and a veil usually forming a ring on the stem.

Agaricus campestris Linnaeus ex Fries –
'Field Mushroom'
> **Cap**: 5–10cm (2–4in)
> **Spores**: deep brown, 6–9 x 4–6μm, smooth
> **Edibility**: edible and delicious, gathered the world over for food

---

One of the most famous edible mushrooms in the world with many common names, including Field Mushrooms, Pink-bottoms and Champignons. This delicious wild mushroom is to be found in large fairy rings in open-grass temperate regions all over the world. The white cap may be smooth to scaly and the crowded gills start bright pink and slowly turn deep brown. The short, stout stem is white with a delicate ring. The white flesh flushes slightly reddish-pink to brown when cut but *not bright yellow* (see *A. xanthoderma* on page 104). The explanations in folklore for fairy rings are quite fascinating and range from fairies dancing to lightning strikes, animals running in circles, witches' cauldrons and buried bodies. In reality they are the natural result of the steady outward growth and expansion of the fungal mycelium, which radiates outwards in a circular fashion and fruits on the actively growing leading edge.

Agaricus cupreobrunneus (Møller) Pilat
> **Cap**: 2.5–7.5cm (1–3in)
> **Spores**: deep brown, 7–9 x 4–6.5μm, smooth
> **Edibility**: edible and good

Less well known than the common Field Mushroom, *A. campestris*, this is nevertheless quite common and equally delicious. It is a short, squat species, much like the field mushroom, but the cap is marked with fine copper-brown to wine-coloured fibres and scales. The young gills start bright pink and soon mature to a deep brown. It likes short grass in open pastures and meadows and may prefer sandy soils.

Agaricus bitorquis (Quélet) Saccardo

Cap: 5–15cm (2–6in)
Spores: deep brown, 5–6 x 4–5μm, smooth
Edibility: edible and good

The way in which mushrooms often push their way up through the hardest of soils is quite remarkable. This species more than any other can be found bursting through hard-packed soil, tarmac or even concrete. Specimens have been seen to push up entire paving slabs through the relentless pressure of osmosis as fluids expand their fruit-bodies upwards. The flattened white cap of this species has extremely thick flesh and only very narrow gills. The stem is thick and heavy and has a curious double ring which leaves a volva-like veil at the base. The flesh slowly stains reddish-brown when cut. Usually found along roadsides, tracks and other disturbed urban areas.

Agaricus bernardii (Quélet) Saccardo

Cap: 12.5–20cm (5–8in)
Spores: deep brown, 5.5–7 x 5–6μm, smooth
Edibility: edible but rather poor

This species takes advantage of areas with high-salt contents, such as seaside pastures, which other species find too inhospitable for growth. It is often very large and robust and the thick-fleshed cap has a deeply in-rolled margin. The very narrow gills are pale greyish-pink before turning deep brown. The short, thick stem has a thick, sheathing ring. The flesh stains quite bright pinkish-red and develops a sour, unpleasant odour with age. As well as its usual coastal habitats it now appears regularly along the edge of roads and it seems likely that the practice of salting roads in winter is producing the correct conditions for fruiting of this normally uncommon species.

Agaricus augustus Fries – 'The Prince'
Cap: 10–25cm (4–10in)
Spores: deep brown, 8–11 x 5–6μm, smooth
Edibility: edible and excellent

In North America this has the common name of Prince, and it is indeed a princely mushroom with its large, golden-tawny cap with fine scales and fibres. The gills are pale pink, maturing to a deep brown. The tall stem is club-shaped and finely woolly-scaly below the large, floppy ring at the top. The mushroom has a very pleasant odour of anise or almonds and is considered one of the very best edible fungi. It often grows in large numbers in woodlands, parks and gardens, usually under shrubs or hedgerows and is one of the most distinctive and easily recognizable species.

Agaricus arvensis Schaeffer ex Secretan – 'Horse Mushroom'
Cap: 10–15cm (4–6in)
Spores: deep brown, 7–9 x 4.5–6μm, smooth
Edibility: edible and excellent

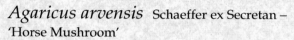

The common name refers to its preference for fields manured with horse dung and to the old practice of cultivating it in trenches filled with soil and horse manure. It is a large, striking species with a white, smooth to scaly cap which ages brassy yellow. The gills are pale pink then deep brown. The club-shaped stem is white with a slightly woolly surface below the ring. The latter is thick and well formed with distinct cogwheel-like scales on the underside. The flesh is white and has a pleasant odour of anise and bruises slight ochre. If brilliant yellow stains develop, be careful; check the description of *A. xanthodermus*, page 104. A common species, it grows in fields and woodland clearings throughout Britain.

Agaricus essettei Bon [=*A. abruptibulbus*, of European authors]
Cap: 7.5–15cm (3–6in)
Spores: deep brown, 6–8 x 4–5μm, smooth
Edibility: edible and good

This is an elegant and rather uncommon species, often confused with the Horse Mushroom. The beautiful white cap bruises brassy yellow and is quite smooth. The gills are very pale pink then mature to a deep brown. The stem is the key feature, since it has a large and very abrupt bulb at the base and is quite smooth overall. There is a large, floppy ring present. The flesh smells pleasantly of anise. It grows in mixed woods, but especially under spruce, and is widespread. The true *A. abruptibulbus* appears to be confined to North America and differs microscopically.

Agaricus silvaticus Schaeffer ex Secretan – 'Red-staining Mushroom'

Cap: 5–10cm (2–4in)
Spores: deep brown, 4.5–6 x 3–3.5μm, smooth
Edibility: edible and quite good

Most species of *Agaricus* stain to some degree, either yellowish or reddish, but in some species this reaches an extreme where the flesh turns either bright red or bright yellow. This species is one of the former, and if the cap or stem is scratched, a bright scarlet stain appears in a few minutes. The cap is a light yellow-brown to russet-brown and covered with fine scales. The gills are pink then dark brown. The slender stem is slightly bulbous and white, and smooth below the fragile ring. It is quite common in coniferous woods throughout Britain. Other red stainers include *A. fuscofibrillosus* with a fibrillose (not scaly) reddish-brown cap, and *A. squamuliferus*, an all-white species. See also *A. haemorrhoidarius*.

Agaricus haemorrhoidarius Kalchbrenner & Schulzer

Cap: 5–10cm (2–4in)
Spores: deep brown, 4.5–6 x 3–4μm
Edibility: edible and quite good

Another species which stains deep red when scratched, this species can be distinguished by its dark, dull brown cap which is densely fibrous-scaly with the scales very indistinct. It is not as clear and attractive as the previous species. The stem is whitish to brown with a slightly felty surface. The ring is marked with woolly brown flecks on the undersurface. This species seems to prefer deciduous woods and is common along shady banks and roadsides under oak and beech.

Agaricus placomyces Peck

Cap: 5–10cm (2–4in)
Spores: deep brown, 5–7 x 3–4μm, smooth
Edibility: inedible and poisonous to many

One of a number of species which bruise bright yellow, especially in the stem base, and which have an unpleasant phenolic odour (rather like iodine or bottles of ink); this can cause painful stomach upsets to many people, although some seem to be unaffected. If you see any bright yellow stains at the stem base, do not risk eating the mushroom. This species has a rounded cap with a flattened centre and is covered with extremely fine grey-black or grey-brown scales. The gills start whitish then mature brown. The elegant stem is bulbous and white with a smooth surface. A floppy ring is present and frequently has brownish droplets on the underside. It grows in woods, hedgerows and gardens, but is not common.

Agaricus xanthodermus Genevier – 'Yellow Stainer'

Cap: 7.5–12.5cm (3–5in)

Spores: deep brown, 5–7 x 3–4µm, smooth

Edibility: poisonous to many, causing nausea and headaches

An infamous mushroom because it is often confused with either the Field Mushroom or the Horse Mushroom, but from both of these it can be easily distinguished if certain key characters are observed: the white cap soon ages greyish and becomes fibrous or scaly, the cap or stem cuticle when scratched, and especially the flesh in the stem base, turn a brilliant chrome-yellow, the flesh has an unpleasant phenolic odour like iodine or old-fashioned school ink, the stem is stout and bulbous and has a well-developed ring with cottony patches on the underside. It seems to frequent urban environments such as hedges, gardens and rubbish tips, but also occurs in woodlands and is quite common. The similar *A. pilatianus* grows in open meadows and fields and is white, smooth to scaly and has a cylindrical or tapering stem base, but also stains bright yellow.

Agaricus lutosus (Møeller) Møeller

Cap: 2.5–5cm (1–2in)

Spores: deep brown, 4.5–5.5 x 3.5–4µm

Edibility: unknown, best avoided

A small and inconspicuous species, it can be quite common in some areas in very short turf, usually on sandy soils. The pale yellowish-brown cap is faintly marked with purplish scales at the centre and may flush completely purplish-brown. The broad gills are pink, then turn pale brown. The short, sturdy stem has a faint ring-zone but is otherwise smooth. All parts bruise a dull yellow-ochre. It smells pleasantly and faintly of anise. This species appears to be identical with *A. micromegathus* Peck, described from North America, and that name has precedence if this is proven.

STROPHARIACEAE
Strophularia Family

A large family with smooth, normally purplish-brown
spores, and gills which are sinuate to adnate and
purplish-brown. A veil is often present, leaving a ring
on the stem, and the cap may be dry to glutinous.

Stropharia coronilla (Bulliard ex Fries) Quélet

Cap: 2.5–5cm (1–2in)
Spores: deep purple-brown, 7–9 x 4–5μm, smooth
Edibility: inedible

This is very often mistaken for a small field
mushroom (*Agaricus*) but the sinuate gills, purplish
spores and yellow-ochre cap colours should all
serve to distinguish it easily. The cap may be quite
viscid when wet and starts pale creamy-yellow, but
ages yellow-ochre to tawny. The short stem is white
with a narrow ring above, often stained purple with
spores. It is a common species in fields and pastures
throughout Britain.

Stropharia thrausta (Schulzer) Saccardo

Cap: 2.5–5cm (1–2in)
Spores: purplish-black, 12–14 x 6–7μm, smooth
Edibility: inedible

This rather rare species is one of the most striking
and attractive to be seen in the autumn woods. The
umbonate cap is a bright fox-red to orange with
small white scales around the margin. The sinuate
gills are purplish-black. The long, elegant stem is
reddish-orange below the narrow ring and whitish
above. It grows in small groups on fallen twigs and
branches of deciduous trees and is widely
distributed. This is very close to the species
S.squamosa, and is regarded simply as a variety by
some authors. *S. squamosa* differs in its convex,
rarely umbonate cap, duller, more ochre-brown
colours but is similar in habitat preferences.

Stropharia semiglobata (Batsch) Quélet
Cap: 2.5–5cm (1–2in)
Spores: purple-brown, 15–19 x 8–10μm, smooth
Edibility: inedible

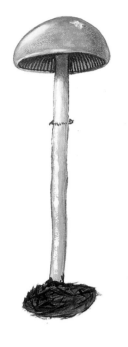

This is sometimes called the Dung Roundhead, which is a good description of both its preferred habitat and its appearance. The small cap is rounded, smooth and very sticky when wet, and a pale to bright yellow-ochre. The adnate gills are deep and a pale lilac-brown. The slender, tall stem is sticky below the narrow ring and coloured like the cap. It grows on horse, sheep and cattle dung everywhere.

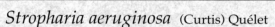

Stropharia aeruginosa (Curtis) Quélet
Cap: 2.5–7.5cm (1–3in)
Spores: violet-brown, 7–9 x 4–5μm, smooth
Edibility: inedible

This could be the archetypal toadstool, with its slimy cap and strange, poisonous-looking colours. However, it does not seem to be particularly poisonous or psychoactive, as is often suggested, but it is certainly of strange appearance. The viscid cap is a bright blue-green with white flecks of veil at the margin. The sinuate gills are a deep violet-brown. The greenish stem is clothed in white scales up to a distinct, well-formed ring. It is a fairly common species late in the season and grows on rich soil or in grass at the edge of woods. The very similar *S. cyanea* differs in having very little white veil, a paler green cap, a thin transient ring and paler gills, and is common in nettle beds, garden borders and woods.

Psilocybe cyanescens Wakefield
Cap: 2.5–7.5cm (1–3in)
Spores: dark purple-brown, 9–12 x 5–7μm, smooth
Edibility: inedible; psychoactive and poisonous

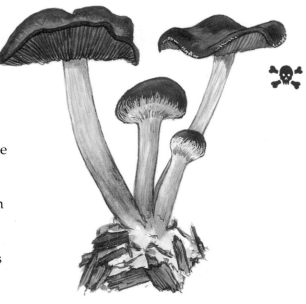

Almost certainly an introduction to Britain from some warmer country, perhaps North America, this species seems to be spreading very rapidly owing to the practice of mulching our gardens with wood chips – its preferred habitat. I have seen a horse ride covered in wood chips along which enormous clumps of this species were fruiting every few inches over a distance of perhaps 45 metres (50 yards) – many thousands of caps. The reddish-brown caps are hygrophanous and rapidly pale at the centre to a dull ochre. The stem is white, tough and fibrous and bruises dull blue with handling or age. As with many *Psilocybe* species, this contains hallucinogenic chemicals, but it also has other toxic side-effects.

Psilocybe semilanceata (Fries ex Secretan)
Kummer – 'Liberty Cap'
    Cap: 0.6–2.5cm (¼–1in)
    Spores: purple-brown, 11–14 x 7–8μm, smooth
    Edibility: inedible; psychoactive and toxic

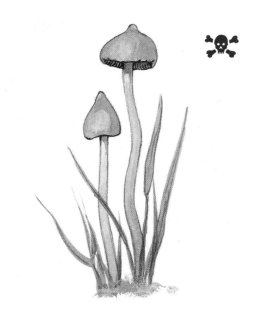

The common name of Liberty Cap refers back to the days of the French Revolution and the tall hats which were in vogue with the revolutionaries at the time. The tall, narrow and sharply pointed caps are pale yellow-buff and sticky in wet weather. The gills are deep grey-brown, then violet-brown. The slender stem is smooth, often twisted and pale yellow, bruising blue. It grows in the depths of old grass tussocks in pastures and fields as well as on lawns in parks and gardens. Widely known because of its hallucinogenic properties.

Hypholoma fasciculare (Hudson ex Fries)
Kummer – 'Sulphur Tuft'
    Cap: 2.5–7.5cm (1–3in)
    Spores: purple-brown, 6.5–8 x 3.5–4μm, smooth
    Edibility: inedible, probably poisonous

One of our commonest fungi, it can be found at almost any time of the year whenever the weather is mild and wet. The clustered caps are smooth and bright yellow-orange when young, becoming pale sulphur-yellow with age. The narrow gills are a distinct greenish-yellow when young but mature to a dull violet-brown. The stems are yellow with a cobwebby veil at the apex. The taste of the flesh is extremely bitter and unpleasant. It grows in large tufts on fallen logs and stumps everywhere.

Hypholoma sublateritium (Fries) Quélet –
'Brick Caps'
    Cap: 5–10cm (2–4in)
    Spores: purple-brown, 6–7 x 4–4.5μm, smooth
    Edibility: edible but not to be confused with
    H. fasciculare, which is toxic

Appearing at the end of the year as the weather turns cooler, the robust caps are indeed a brick-red with paler veil remnants at the margin. The gills are whitish-yellow, then grey-violet. The thick stems are pale brick-red with a cobwebby veil at the apex. It grows in tufts on fallen timber and is quite common throughout Britain.

COPRINACEAE
Coprinus Family

Usually thin, delicate mushrooms (there are exceptions), they all have black spores and many species have a veil and/or a ring. *Coprinus* species are often called ink caps because they dissolve away into an inky liquid as they disperse their spores.

Panaeolus sphinctrinus (Fries) Quélet
Cap: 2.5–5cm (1–2in)
Spores: blackish, 13–16 x 8–11μm, smooth
Edibility: inedible

A relatively small group of species, the majority of which grow in grass, often on animal dung. This species has a silvery-grey to yellow-grey cap which is bell-shaped, and when young and fresh has tiny white 'teeth' which are veil remnants around the margin. The gills are greyish and, like all *Panaeolus* species, become mottled with black as the spores mature in irregular patches. The slender stem is smooth and pale grey. It grows on horse or cow dung everywhere.

Panaeolus semiovatus (Sowerby ex Fries)
Lundell & Nannfeldt
Cap: 2.5–7.5cm (1–3in)
Spores: blackish, 15–20 x 8–11μm, smooth
Edibility: inedible

One of the largest members of the group, although very variable in size, as are all fungi which grow on dung. The bell-shaped cap is pale buff to whitish and slightly sticky when wet. It frequently cracks in dry weather. The gills are widely spaced, blackish-grey and mottled. The tall stem is rigid, with a distinct ring at the apex which soon vanishes with age. It seems to prefer horse dung and is widespread throughout Britain.

Panaeolus foenisecii (Persoon ex Fries) Maire
Cap: 1–2.5cm (½—1in)
Spores: purple-brown, 12–15 x 6.5–9μm, with minute warts
Edibility: inedible

An extremely common mushroom, there can hardly be a lawn anywhere that has not had this mushroom growing on it at one time or another. The rounded to flattened cap starts date-brown but rapidly dries to a pale pinkish-buff. The widely spaced gills are dark brown. The slender stem is pale buff. There is some debate as to which genus to place this mushroom in since it is atypical for a *Panaeolus* in having warty spores. You may see it listed as a *Panaeolina*, or even a *Psathyrella*.

Psathyrella candolleana (Fries) R. Maire

Cap: 2.5–7.5cm (1–3in)

Spores: purplish-brown, 7–10 x 4–5μm, almost cylindrical, smooth

Edibility: inedible

Almost a 'weed' species in some areas, this mushroom appears close to stumps and buried wood everywhere. The extremely fragile caps are soon expanded and buff-brown, drying rapidly to ivory-white. The narrow gills are greyish-lilac. The slender stems are white and it grows in small tufts. There is no obvious veil present, unlike some other closely related species such as *P. leucotephra*.

Psathyrella velutina (Persoon ex Fries)
Singer [=*Lacrymaria lacrymabunda*]

Cap: 2.5–7.5cm (1–3in)

Spores: blackish-brown, 9–12 x 6–7μm, warty

Edibility: edible but best avoided

Extremely common along tracks and paths in woodlands and wherever the soil has been disturbed. The pale reddish-brown cap is fibrous-hairy and frequently ragged at the margin. The gills are deep yellow, then black with white edges, and often weep droplets of liquid. The shaggy stem is also reddish-brown and has a ring zone at the top. The similar but rarer *P. pyrotricha* is much brighter reddish-orange and prefers spruce woods.

Psathyrella hydrophila (Bulliard ex Merat)
R. Maire

Cap: 2–5cm (1–2in)

Spores: black-brown, 4.5–7 x 3–4μm

Edibility: inedible

A very fragile species that is difficult to collect intact, it grows in quite large clumps. The cap is very hygrophanous and starts chestnut-brown before drying to a pale ochre-buff from the centre outwards. There are obvious veil remnants left at the cap margin. The gills are narrow and pale brown to chestnut. The thin stems are hollow, white and brittle. It frequents stumps and woody debris in deciduous woods.

Coprinus picaceus (Bulliard) Fries – 'Magpie'

Cap: 5–10cm (2–4in high)
Spores: black, 14–19 x 10–13μm, smooth
Edibility: doubtful, best avoided

The common name describes the strikingly patched
and spotted appearance of the cap when the
originally uniform, fleecy white veil splits to reveal
the blackish undersurface. As it ages, the lower edge
of the cap deliquesces (dissolves away) and
continues upwards until only a tiny fragment of cap
is left perched on the tall, white stem. It is an
uncommon species, preferring chalky soils under
beech trees in southern England. This is one of the
few *Coprinus* species (see also *C. atramentarius*) that
has been reported to cause poisoning, and is thus
best avoided. A sort of miniature look-alike of this
species is *C. episcopalis*, which also grows in beech-
wood leaf litter, but has a small, marginate bulb at
the stem base.

Coprinus comatus (Müller ex Fries)
S. F. Gray – 'Shaggy Mane'; 'Lawyer's Wig'

Cap: 5–10cm (2–4in tall)
Spores: black, 11–15 x 6–8.5μm, smooth
Edibility: edible and delicious when young

This species is well known enough to have received
several common names, very unusual for a
mushroom. Both of the names given allude to the
white, shaggy surface of the cap where each scale
recurves back to look very like the curls on a
lawyer's wig. As in the previous species, and,
indeed, all *Coprinus* species, the cap rapidly dissolves
away from the margin upwards so as to release the
spores. The tall white stem is smooth and has a thin
white ring around the middle. It grows in grass and
bare soil wherever there has been disturbance and is
very common along roadsides and freshly laid
lawns, as well as rubbish dumps and landfills. The
'ink' of this species, and others, has been used in
times past quite literally as writing ink, and its use is
detectable by the dried spores preserved on the
paper or parchment. It makes a good ink, but
without preservatives rapidly becomes very smelly!

Coprinus atramentarius (Bulliard ex Fries) Fries

Cap: 2.5–5cm (1–2in)
Spores: black, 7–11 x 4–6μm, smooth
Edibility: edible, except with alcohol

A remarkable species which typifies a reaction known only in a very few mushrooms. If eaten alone, it generally causes no problems, but if consumed with alcohol, an unpleasant reaction of palpitations, nausea, tingling and flushing of the extremities occurs. The chemical which causes this is very similar to that used in the treatment of alcoholism – Antabuse. This common species grows in large clumps near stumps and buried wood everywhere, and has a grey-brown, slightly scaly cap with a white, spindle-shaped stem with a distinct ring zone-close to the base.

Coprinus micaceus (Bulliard ex Fries) Fries

Cap: 2.5–3.5cm (1–3in)
Spores: black, 7–10 x 4–5μm, smooth
Edibility: edible but poor

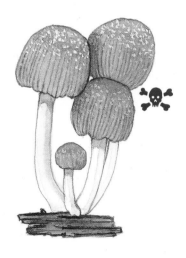

A beautiful species when young and viewed through a lens, for the entire cap is coated with a fine layer of reflective, mica-like cells over the reddish-brown surface. As it expands, the margin becomes strongly striate-pleated. The whitish stems are joined into large clusters. It grows at the base of stumps and buried wood everywhere.

Coprinus plicatilis (Curtis ex Fries) Fries

Cap: 0.6–2.5 (¼–1in)
Spores: black, 10–13 x 6.5–10μm, smooth
Edibility: inedible

A beautiful, tiny and delicate species looking just like an oriental parasol. The cap flattens out and is deeply pleated and furrowed radially. The narrow gills are separated from the stem by a narrow collar. The extremely fragile stem is whitish. The entire mushroom lasts only a few hours, although it hardly deliquesces (dissolves), merely collapsing with age. It is very common in fields and lawns everywhere.

PAXILLACEAE
Paxillus Family

This group, despite their gills, are thought to be closely related to the boletes. They share many microscopic and chemical features and have similar spore colours.

Paxillus involutus (Bataille ex Fries) Fries

Cap: 5–15cm (2–6in)

Spores: ochre-brown, 7–9 x 4–6µm, smooth

Edibility: poisonous if eaten raw or inadequately cooked, and has proved deadly to some. It may have a cumulative toxic effect

Until recent years this was not suspected of being poisonous and, indeed, many people in Europe ate it regularly. But then suspicion fell upon it in a number of deaths and it now appears to be cumulatively deadly in its effects. The poisoning seems to be increased when eaten raw or incorrectly cooked. On no account should this now be eaten. The ochre-brown cap has a strongly in-rolled, woolly margin when young and can be quite viscid when wet. This soon flattens out, leaving a rather grooved margin. The soft, crowded gills are yellowish and bruise quickly rust-brown. The short stem is smooth and coloured like the cap. It is often abundant in mixed woods, especially birch, throughout Britain.

Paxillus atrotomentosus (Bataille ex Fries) Fries

Cap: 5–20cm (2–8in)

Spores: yellowish-brown, 5–6 x 3–4µm, smooth

Edibility: supposedly edible but best avoided in view of its relationship to *P. involutus*, described above

This often huge mushroom grows only on dead stumps of pine trees and is common throughout most of Britain. The stem is extremely short and usually offset to one side of the large, brownish cap. The gills are crowded, soft and yellow. The flesh is yellow to pinkish and rather bitter.

Phylloporus rhodoxanthus (Schweinitz) Bresadola

Cap: 2.5–10cm (1–4in)

Spores: olive-brown, 9–12 x 3–5µm, spindle shaped

Edibility: edible but poor

This looks remarkably like some of the boletes, such as *B. subtomentosus*, until you turn it over and realize that it has gills. In almost all characteristics, macroscopic, microscopic and chemical, it shows relationships with the boletes. The velvety reddish-yellow to brown cap gives a brilliant green reaction with ammonia, just like some of the boletes. The gills are bright yellow, thick and often poorly formed, with strong cross-veins almost like shallow tubes, and are easily separated from the cap just like the tubes of the boletes. In this country it is rather rare and grows in mixed woods, mainly in southern England.

CORTINARIACEAE
Cortinarius Family

This is the largest family of mushrooms in the world, particularly the genus *Cortinarius*, and they grow in a bewildering number of forms, colours and sizes. The spores vary from rust-brown to dull cigar-brown and may be smooth, warty or even angular-lumpy. A cobwebby veil is often present. Some *Cortinarius* species are now known to be deadly poisonous and all should be avoided for culinary purposes.

Cortinarius trivialis Lange
Cap: 5–10cm (2–4in)
Spores: rust-brown, 10–15 x 7–8μm, warty
Edibility: inedible

Swamps and bogs are wonderful places to hunt mushrooms, and many *Cortinarius* species, including this one, prefer to grow in such habitats. It particularly likes willow bogs. The very viscid cap is yellow-brown, while the gills are pale lilac before turning rust-brown from the mature spores. The stem is peculiarly banded and zoned with viscid rings of whitish-yellow veil over a darker brown background. The flesh is white with pale lilac in the stem apex.

Cortinarius muscigenus Peck
[=*C.collinitus* of some authors]
Cap: 5–10cm (2–4in)
Spores: rust-brown, 12–15 x 7–8μm, warty
Edibility: inedible

Many *Cortinarius* species have some blue or violet colours in the stem or gills, and in this species the entire stem is flushed violet and banded with thicker rings of viscid veil. The viscid cap is a rich orange to tawny-brown, while the gills are white at first then rust-brown. It also likes boggy situations and is quite common and widespread. Although until recently known by the name *C. collinitus*, it has been shown that this is a confused concept, not really referring to this species, so that name has to be rejected. Since the same species was also described from North America under the name *C. muscigenus*, that name is available and has been adopted.

Cortinarius pseudosalor Lange

Cap: 5–10cm (2–4in)
Spores: rust-brown
Edibility: inedible

This species can be found in beech woods almost anywhere in Britain and at times may be the commonest species present. The viscid cap is strangely wrinkled and radially ridged and is a pale ochre-brown. The gills are a pale clay-buff when young, then rust-brown. The spindle-shaped stem is often rooted into the soil, is usually bluish-lilac and viscid up to a distinct ring zone, and white above.

Cortinarius delibutus Fries

Cap: 5–10cm (2–4in)
Spores: rust-brown, 7–8 x 5–6µm, warty
Edibility: inedible

Another species which prefers boggy, mossy areas, especially under birch and willow. The sticky, rounded cap is a bright yellow-ochre, while the young gills and apex of the stem are a pale lavender. The lower half of the stem is also sticky and is a pale yellow with darker yellow bands. The stickiness is actually a complete veil (the universal veil) which enveloped the young mushroom. There is also a cobwebby partial veil present at the top of the stem. This species is very distinctive for its almost globose spores.

Cortinarius croceocaeruleus (Persoon) Fries

Cap: 2.5–5cm (1–2in)
Spores: rust-brown, 7.5–8.5µm, warty
Edibility: inedible

A rather small species in this group with both sticky cap and stem and very attractive with its pale bluish-lilac colours. The colour in the cap soon fades, however, and becomes a dull ochre with a bluish margin. The stem is spindle-shaped and white to pale ochre. The taste is distinctly bitter, while the odour is a pleasant one of honey. Fairly common late in the year, it is found only under beech trees on chalky soils in southern England.

Cortinarius volvatus   A. H. Smith

Cap: 5–10cm (2–4in)
Spores: rust-brown, 8–10.5 x 5–6μm, warty
Edibility: inedible

Although all *Cortinarius* species have a veil of sorts it is rarely well developed and so it is all the more striking when it occurs, as in this species, in the form of a volva-like structure on the stem. The cap is bluish and viscid when young, then browner and dry with age, while the young gills are deep blue-violet. The stem is bluish and dry, and very bulbous but the edge of the bulb has thick, soft remnants of an enveloping white veil which stand up to form a volva or sac. The taste is bitter. Only recently discovered in Britain (it was described in North America), it is a rare species found under beech on chalky soils in southern England.

Cortinarius sodagnitus   Henry

Cap: 5–10cm (2–4in)
Spores: rust-brown, 10–12 x 5.5–6.5μm, warty
Edibility: inedible

One of the most beautiful of all mushrooms – many people never imagine that such colours can be present in 'lowly' fungi. The viscid cap, dry stem and gills are all of the brightest and most intense violet. As it ages, the violet slowly fades to brown. The stem is very bulbous with a distinct, gutter-like upper margin. The taste of the cap skin is bitter, while the flesh is mild. If a drop of caustic soda (KOH) is placed on the cap, it turns a brilliant scarlet. It is quite common in some years under beech on chalk in southern England. The similar *C. dibaphus* is also violet but is bitter in both cuticle and flesh and the KOH reaction is pink instead of scarlet.

Cortinarius auroturbinatus   (Secretan) Lange

Cap: 5–10cm (2–4in)
Spores: rust-brown, 12–15 x 7–8μm, very warty
Edibility: inedible

There are a number of brilliant yellow or orange species in this section, often difficult to separate, of which this is perhaps the most common. The rounded cap is a bright golden-yellow viscid when young, and flushing more tawny-orange with age. The gills are bright yellow when young, then soon rust-brown. The bulbous stem is whitish-yellow with a prominent cobwebby veil when young. If caustic soda (KOH) is placed on the cap, a red-brown to purplish stain is produced. As with most of the species in this group, it prefers beech trees on chalky soils in the south.

Cortinarius purpurascens Fries

Cap: 5–10cm (2–4in)

Spores: rust-brown, 8–10 x 4–5.5µm, warty

Edibility: inedible

Colour changes in the flesh are not as common in species of *Cortinarius* as in some other groups, but in this species it is very noticeable and diagnostic. All parts of the mushroom bruise a deep purple-violet, especially the gills and stem. The slightly sticky cap is dark brown streaked with darker fibres and can show violet flushes at the margin. The gills and stem are pale violet and the stem has a distinctly bulbous base. It is a fairly common species in mixed woods throughout Britain.

Cortinarius torvus (Fries) Fries

Cap: 5–10cm (2–4in)

Spores: rust-brown, 8–10 x 5–6µm, warty

Edibility: inedible

There are an enormous number of small to medium-sized species with brown colours, and dry cap and stem, differing in minor macroscopic and microscopic characters, and for the most part very specialized literature is required to identify them. This is one of the few which stands out by means of some distinctive feature. It might be given the common name of 'Stocking Cortinarius' because the club-shaped stem really does look as if it has a whitish stocking pulled halfway up. This is the remains of the universal veil. The widely spaced gills and the apex of the stem are violet when young. It is a common species in beech woods throughout Britain.

Cortinarius armillatus (Fries) Fries

Cap: 5–10cm (2–4in)

Spores: rust-brown, 9–12 x 5.5–7.5µm, warty

Edibility: inedible

This may be the easiest of all *Cortinarius* to identify, and even complete beginners quickly learn to recognize it. The very bulbous stem has 1–3 bright cinnabar-red bands of veil circling the stem, which is otherwise smooth and pale whitish-brown. The cap is a rich brick-red, dry and fibrous. When very young it can look very strange, with tiny button cap perched upon an enormous rounded bulb. It can grow in large circles in beech and birch woods and is quite common.

Cortinarius evernius (Fries) Fries

Cap: 5–10cm (2–4in)
Spores: rust-brown, 9–11 x 5–6μm, warty
Edibility: inedible

This mushroom can be extremely beautiful, particularly when young and the colours are most intense. The entire mushroom is a clear blue-violet with bands of white veil on the tall, elegant stem. The cap gradually darkens to a deep reddish-brown. It grows in *Sphagnum* moss in pine woods, and like all species which grow in such deep mosses, the stems can elongate enormously in a bid to push through the moss. The size, therefore, can vary considerably and allowance must be made for this when trying to identify it.

Cortinarius alboviolaceus (Persoon ex Fries) Fries

Cap: 5–10cm (2–4in)
Spores: rust-brown, 8–10 x 5–6μm, warty
Edibility: inedible

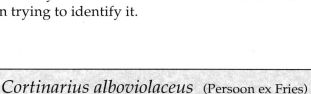

The Latin name means whitish-violet and is a good description of the overall colours of this species. The entire mushroom is silvery-white with a flush of lavender or violet. The bulbous stem is ringed or booted with a white veil over the lower half. The flesh is violet above fading to pale ochre below. It is one of our commoner species and grows in beech woods throughout Britain.

Cortinarius argentatus (Persoon ex Fries) Fries

Cap: 5–10cm (2–4in)
Spores: rust-brown, 8–10 x 5–6μm, warty
Edibility: inedible

Another silvery-white to lavender species, this differs from the previous one in its almost total lack of a veil and the distinctly bulbous stem base. With age the lavender colours fade from the cap to be replaced by pale ochre, and old specimens may be completely ochre. It is not a common species but in some years may appear in large numbers in beech woods in southern England.

Cortinarius violaceus (Fries) S. F. Gray
Cap: 5–10cm (2–4in)
Spores: rust-brown, 13–17 x 8–10μm, warty
Edibility: inedible

Sadly, this is a rather rare mushroom in Britain, for it is one of the most intensely coloured of all mushrooms. The entire body is the deepest violet, often almost blackish it is so dark. The cap is dry and minutely scaly, while the stem is fibrous. It seems to prefer beech or birch woods and has been reported as fruiting for only a very short time each year, which may account for its being seen so rarely.

Cortinarius bolaris (Persoon ex Fries) Fries
Cap: 5–7.5cm (2–3in)
Spores: rust-brown, 6–7 x 5–6μm, warty
Edibility: poisonous; suspected of being deadly

One of the relatively few species of *Cortinarius* which stains with age or handling, the pale yellowish cap and stem become spotted with copper-red scales. Eventually the entire mushroom will turn a dull copper-red to brick-red. It is a fairly common species in beech woods throughout Britain. Like a number of other species, it is now suspected of being a dangerously poisonous mushroom, and as with all other members of this genus, must be avoided as an edible.

Cortinarius rubellus Cooke
[=*C. speciosissimus*]
Cap: 2.5–7.5cm (1–3in)
Spores: rust-brown, 8–11 x 6.5–8.5μm, warty
Edibility: deadly poisonous; causes severe kidney damage and possible death

For many years *Cortinarius* were considered to be 'safe' if not particularly exciting edibles. But a series of poisonings in Europe led to the implication of this and other species, particularly *C. orellanus*, in a number of poisonings and deaths. It is now known that they contain a series of complex toxins grouped together under the name orellanin. They are particularly dangerous in that many days may pass before symptoms become evident, by which time great damage to the kidneys may have already occurred. This species is rare in Britain, being found mostly in the north under conifers, often in moss. It has bands of veil remnants on the stem and a smell of radish. The similar but very rare *C. orellanus*, which has been seen only in the south, has a rounded, not umbonate cap, no veil remnants on the stem and narrower spores.

Cortinarius traganus (Fries) Fries

Cap: 5–10cm (2–4in)
Spores: rust-brown, 7–10 x 5–6µm, warty
Edibility: inedible

This beautiful fungus has a most penetrating and usually unpleasant odour. The entire mushroom is a clear lilac-lavender with whitish veil remnants spread over the cap and stem. The flesh is a bright yellow-brown and usually marbled irregularly. All parts of the mushroom emit a strong, pungent odour variously described as over-ripe pears, goats or acetylene gas. It is a frequent species in the pine woods of Scotland and cannot easily be mistaken for anything else.

Cortinarius sanguineus (von Wulfen) Fries

Cap: 2.5–5cm (1–2in)
Spores: rust-brown, 6–9 x 4–6µm, warty
Edibility: suspect; possibly poisonous

Such an intense blood-red to carmine-red is very rare in mushrooms, only commonly being seen in the caps of species of *Russula*. Here, however, the entire mushroom is coloured both inside and out. This is quite a common species under conifers in Britain. A form with traces of golden veil and perhaps more purple-red colours is found under deciduous trees and is often called *C. puniceus* Orton. This and the following species are placed, along with a number of other species, in a separate subgenus called *Dermocybe*, distinguished by their bright colours – either reds or greenish-yellows – and their unusual chemistry.

Cortinarius semisanguineus (Fries) Gillet

Cap: 2.5–5cm (1–2in)
Spores: rust-brown, 6–8 x 4–5µm, warty
Edibility: suspect, possibly poisonous

One of the commonest members in this group, the cap is a rather dull ochre-brown, as is the stem, but turn it over and the vivid blood-red to cinnabar-red gills are revealed. This and other species in the same group are greatly valued for use in the dyeing of wool, yielding beautiful yellow, gold and reddish pigments. Many other fungi can also be used for dyeing, and give colours ranging from palest lavender to violet, browns, greens and even blue. Several books are now available on this fascinating hobby.

Hebeloma crustuliniforme
(Bulliard ex St Amans) Quélet – 'Poison Pie'
> **Cap**: 5–10cm (2–4in)
> **Spores**: dull cinnamon-brown, 9–13 x 5.5–7µm,
> minutely warty
> **Edibility**: poisonous; causes severe stomach upsets

The cap of this and related species do indeed look
rather like a pie, although the pastry is apparently
uncooked. The entire mushroom is a pale ivory-buff,
like unbaked dough. The gills are pale grey-brown
to tan and the edges are often beaded with tiny
droplets. There is a strong odour of radish and the
taste is slightly bitter. It is a common species late in
the year in mixed woods everywhere.

Hebeloma edurum Metrod ex Bon
> **Cap**: 5–15cm (2–6in)
> **Spores**: dull cinnamon-brown, 9–12 x 5–7µm,
> minutely warty
> **Edibility**: poisonous; causes severe stomach upsets

Rather a large species, the cap is a dull ochre-brown to beige
with a slightly furrowed margin. The gills are pale buff and
do not weep droplets, unlike some other species. The stout
stem is fibrous-scaly with a slight ring-zone, and tends to
stain brown at the base. The odour is pleasant, of fruit or
chocolate, then slowly becomes unpleasant. It prefers conifer
woods on chalky soils and is very uncommon in Britain.

Hebeloma radicosum (Bulliard) Ricken
> **Cap**: 7.5–12.5cm (3–5in)
> **Spores**: pale brown, 9–10 x 5–6µm, minutely warty
> **Edibility**: inedible, possibly poisonous

This fascinating species has a unique lifestyle as well as a
wonderful odour. Like a small number of other closely related
species, it seems to require soil with a high nitrogen content in
order to grow. In this instance, if the long-rooting stem is traced
down through the soil, it will almost invariably be found to arise
from the burrow of an animal. Animal burrows are usually
enriched with nitrogen because of their urine and droppings. I
have even found this species emerging from a kingfisher burrow.
Related species are found around the decaying remains of dead
animals and have been given the name of Ghoul Fungus. Once
again, the extra nitrogen seems to be the reason for this strange
association. The slightly scaly, dull clay-coloured cap of this species
emits the most wonderful odour of marzipan or bitter almonds.

This species is sometimes given the common name of Gypsy, a reference to the fine, frost-like traces of white veil which are left on the cap as it expands. When very young this white veil may be tinted with lavender. The cap has a finely radially wrinkled surface and the gills are pale buff and join the stem. The stem is cylindrical, fibrous and has a white ring around the centre, often stained brown from fallen spores. It is sadly rare in Britain, being confined to the Scottish Highlands in conifer woods.

The genus *Inocybe* is closely related to *Cortinarius* shown in the previous pages, but has a much darker, duller brown spore colour and the mushrooms themselves tend to be rather dull and featureless for the most part. There are numerous species and most are difficult to distinguish without a microscope. Most *Inocybe* species have very well developed cystidia on the gill margin and some of these have strange crystals at the apex. This species has a rounded, scaly, dark brown cap and stem, but usually dark blue-green stains at the stem base. It grows in mossy areas under conifers and is not uncommon. The spores are smooth and elliptical, whereas some *Inocybe* species have strange, knobbly or irregular-shaped spores. The marginal cystidia are short and club-shaped.

Quite an attractive species for an *Inocybe*, this has a pale cap with darker, flattened scales. The stem is silky-fibrous and cylindrical and like the cap, it soon stains dull red if scratched. The gills and flesh have a strong, sweet to unpleasant smell of ripe pears. It is fairly common and seems to like heavy, clay soils under deciduous trees. There is a variety, *pisciodora*, which has a strong smell of fish. The marginal cystidia are long and club-shaped.

Inocybe patouillardii Bresadola
Cap: 5–10cm (2–4in)
Spores: deep brown, 10–13 x 5.5–7µm, bean-shaped
Edibility: dangerously poisonous

This is an infamous species and has caused some serious poisonings in the past. This is presumably because it is an essentially white mushroom which is sometimes confused with the Field Mushroom, although in its other features it is very different. The fibrous, pointed cap and tough, fibrous stem bruise bright red then dull brick red. The odour is heavy and rather earthy or fruity. The gills are white at first, then soon greyish-ochre. It is fairly uncommon and grows quite early in the season in open grassy woodlands on chalky soils.

Inocybe pyriodora (Persoon ex Fries) Quélet
Cap: 5–7.5cm (2–3in)
Spores: dull brown, 7–10 x 5–7.5µm, elliptical
Edibility: poisonous

Inocybe is rich in species with unusual odours, and a number of them have strong fruit smells of one kind or another. In this instance the smell of pears is very strong. It is otherwise distinguished by its pinkish-ochre or yellow-brown fibrous, domed cap which bruises slightly pinkish-red. The stem is pale brown and fibrous to slightly shaggy. It is quite common in deciduous woods and widespread.

Inocybe geophylla (Bulliard) Karsten
Cap: 1–2.5cm (½–1in)
Spores: dull brown, 7–9 x 4–5.5µm, elliptical
Edibility: poisonous

A pretty little species which comes in a number of distinct colour forms, from white through pink to pale lavender, each of which have been given their own varietal names by various authorities. The cap and stem are both smooth and silky, and the mushroom has a strong earthy odour. It can be very common and grows in small troops in mixed woods throughout Britain.

Gymnopilus junonius (Fries) Orton
[=*G. spectabilis*]
Cap: 7.5–15cm (3–6in)
Spores: bright orange-brown, 8–10 x 5–6µm, coarsely warty
Edibility: inedible, very bitter

A spectacular species growing in large clumps, the caps are bright orange-tawny and become coarsely fibrous and scaly with age. The gills are crowded, shallow, orange to rust-brown and often speckled. The tough, large stem is swollen, spindle-shaped to club-shaped and has a well-developed membranous ring. The flesh is yellowish and extremely bitter to taste. It grows attached to buried wood or on fallen logs and stumps of deciduous trees.

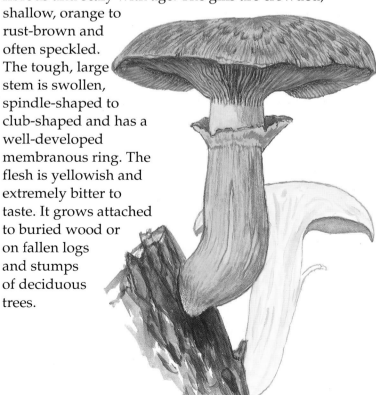

Kuehneromyces mutabilis (Schaeffer)
Singer & Smith [=*Galerina mutabilis*]
> **Cap**: 2.5–7.5cm (1–3in)
> **Spores**: ochre-brown, 6–7 x 3–4.5μm, smooth to slightly warty
> **Edibility**: edible and good, but see warning below

This is a species which has undergone several name changes because authorities are undecided which genus it belongs to; it has also been placed in *Pholiota*. Whatever its name, it is an attractive and delicious species with a sticky cap when wet which characteristically fades at the centre as it dries. The scaly stem has a distinct ring at the top and the gills are rust-brown. It grows in large clumps on dead wood in deciduous woods and is quite common late in the year. Although it is an excellent edible, care must be taken not to confuse it with some *Galerina* species, such as *G. marginata*, and one or two others which are deadly poisonous. They usually become paler from the edge inwards, are more fragile and usually striate, and their spores are distinctly warted. Their stems do not have small recurved scales.

Galerina marginata (Fries) Kuehner
> **Cap**: 2.5–5cm (1–2in)
> **Spores**: rust-brown
> **Edibility**: deadly poisonous

There have, fortunately, been very few cases of poisoning by this species, probably because it is rather small and not particularly attractive or appetizing in appearance. The flattened cap is dark tawny-brown, slightly sticky when wet but soon dry, and often has a striate margin. The gills are adnate, crowded and rust-brown. The stem is smooth, minutely lined and has a delicate ring above. It grows in small clumps on fallen logs, especially conifers, and is locally common. It contains similar toxins to those found in the Death Cap, *Amanita phalloides*, and causes severe liver damage with vomiting, diarrhoea, hypothermia and eventual death if treatment is not rapidly administered.

Phaeocollybia lugubris (Fries) Heim
> **Cap**: 5–7.5cm (2–3in)
> **Spores**: dull brown, 7–9 x 4–5μm, warty
> **Edibility**: uncertain; best avoided

Some of the fungi shown in this book are uncommon to rare and this is one of the rarest. It is included because it is unusual and distinctive and because we know very little about its distribution. It also adds some excitement to a search for a rare species in a likely habitat. The bluntly conical cap is reddish-brown to olive-brown with an irregular lobed margin. The gills are pale orange-ochre. The stem is smooth, deeply rooting and whitish-brown, flushed pinkish below. The flesh is pale with an odour of radish. It is a member of a group of species which are much commoner in North America and northern Europe than in Britain; here it seems confined to conifer woods – especially spruce – in the north.

STROPHARIACEAE
Stropharia Family

Most species grow on or near wood and may have glutinous, dry or scaly caps. The gills are sinuate-adnate and the spores are yellow-brown to rust-brown and smooth. Usually a veil and/or ring is present.

Pholiota lenta (Persoon) Singer
Cap: 5–10cm (2–4in)
Spores: ochre-brown, 6–7 x 3–4μm, smooth
Edibility: inedible

Unlike most *Pholiota* species, this one prefers to grow on the ground in woody debris in leaf litter. The pallid, yellow-beige cap is very viscid and has tiny white veil flakes floating in the slime. The gills are pale cinnamon to rust. The stem is whitish with woolly scales up to a faint ring-zone. There is a slight odour of straw, and the taste is mild. It is a fairly common species in beech woods and usually appears rather late in the year.

Pholiota squarrosa (Müller) Kummer
Cap: 5–15cm (2–6in)
Spores: ochre-brown, 6–8 x 3–4μm, smooth
Edibility: inedible, possibly mildly poisonous

Certainly one of the scaliest mushrooms around, it can be quite spectacular to find a large clump of this species in good condition. Both the cap and the stem, which are dry, are covered in small, pointed and recurved scales. The colour varies from tawny-yellow to russet on a paler background. The crowded gills are yellow to slightly olive, then rust-brown. The flesh is yellowish with a strong, straw-like odour and tastes rather bitter. It is a common species growing at the base of deciduous trees and stumps. There is some doubt as to whether this species is poisonous or not, most reports calling it edible but poor, but there have been some reports of mild poisoning. Such cases may be a case of individual susceptibility, or allergic reaction, but it is in any case best avoided.

Pholiota flammans (Fries) Kummer

Cap: 2.5–7.5cm (1–3in)

Spores: ochre-brown, 4–5 x 2.5–3μm, smooth

Edibility: doubtful; best avoided

The specific name describes the species well: 'flame-coloured' *Pholiota* is a good description. It is perhaps the brightest of all the species in Europe, its cap a brilliant golden-yellow to orange with paler yellow, pointed scales. The cap cuticle is sticky below the scales. The stem is densely scaly up to the ring zone and is dry. The flesh is bright yellow with a fruity odour and rather acrid, unpleasant flavour. It is quite common and grows in small clusters on fallen conifer logs and stumps, especially in Scotland.

Pholiota aurivella (Fries) Kummer

Cap: 5–15cm (2–5in)

Spores: ochre-brown, 7–10 x 4.5–6μm, smooth

Edibility: doubtful; best avoided

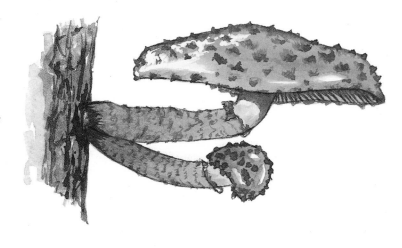

This very glutinous species usually grows on standing trees, occasionally on fallen logs, and is often to be seen emerging from an old knot-hole or wound in the trunk of a beech tree. The bright orange cap is viscid with small, dark brown, glutinous scales which can wash off in rainy weather. The gills are crowded and pale yellow to tawny. The stem, in contrast to the cap, is dry with small, yellowish recurved scales.The flesh is yellowish and mild to taste. It is quite common, especially late in the year, and is widespread throughout Britain.

Pholiota highlandensis (Peck) Smith & Hesler [=*P. carbonaria* of older British literature]

Cap: 2.5–5cm (1–2in)

Spores: ochre-brown, 5–8 x 3.5–4.5μm, smooth

Edibility: doubtful; best avoided

This is one of a number of fungi which specialize in old burn-sites around dead stumps and which move in rapidly to colonize the area for a couple of years before the site eventually grows over and returns to normal. This species has a tawny-brown sticky cap which is smooth and without scales. The gills are yellowish to rust and slightly adnate-decurrent. The stem is tawny and slightly fibrous up to a whitish-yellow ring zone. Wherever a forest fire has occurred this species may be found a year or two later.

Pholiota alnicola (Fries) Singer

Cap: 5–10cm (2–4in)

Spores: ochre-brown, 7.5–11 x 4.5–5.5μm, smooth

Edibility: doubtful; best avoided

With its smooth, yellow cap and elegant stature, this can be mistaken for the Sulphur Tuft Mushroom, *Hypholoma fasciculare*, but that species has purple-brown spores and is much more fragile. This mushroom has a whitish-lavender veil which leaves tiny remnants hanging on the cap margin and has a ring zone at the stem apex. It grows in clumps, usually around the base of dead trees, especially birch and alder, and is quite common in some areas. Its strong, fragrant odour is another useful characteristic. Similar species are *P. flavida*, which is also bright yellow but odourless and grows on conifers, and *P. connisans*, which is smaller, pale clay-ochre in colour and grows on willows.

Pholiota gummosa (Lasch) Singer

Cap: 2.5–7.5cm (1–3in)

Spores: rust-brown, 6–8 x 4–5μm, smooth

Edibility: doubtful; best avoided

A rather small and inconspicuous species, it is nevertheless quite attractive. The sticky cap is pale straw-yellow with small, whitish scales at the margin. The gills are straw to ochre-brown and the stem is coloured like the cap and has woolly, whitish scales up to a distinct ring zone. It grows on buried wood in small clumps and seems to prefer heavy, clay soils. It is quite common. Also on the ground, particularly in damp grass under alder or willow, can be found *P. abstrusa*. This is about the same size as *P. gummosa*, but differs in its yellower cap, which is finely fibrous to lightly sticky, and its yellow, silky stem.

BOLBITIACEAE
Bolbitius Family

The cap cuticle of these fungi is made up of
rounded rather than thread-like cells, and all
have pale brown spores.

Bolbitius vitellinus (Persoon ex Fries) Fries
Cap: 2–5cm (¾–2in)
Spores: rust-ochre, 10–15 x 6–9µm, smooth
Edibility: inedible

Some fungi are so fragile that they are almost
impossible to collect without damage, and this one
falls into that category. The beautiful lemon-yellow
cap is very viscid and deeply grooved when old. The
thin, elegant stem is white with a minutely hairy
surface and snaps very easily. The mushroom tends
to collapse and partially dissolve with age, and
rarely lasts much more than a few hours. It grows on
rich soil wherever there is dung, manure or rotted
straw, and is common everywhere.

Agrocybe praecox (Persoon) Fayod
Cap: 2.5–7.5cm (1–3in)
Spores: dull, tobacco-brown, 8–11 x 5–6µm, smooth
Edibility: inedible, tasteless but apparently not
poisonous

The name *praecox* means 'early' and refers to the
time of year when this and some related species
prefer to grow. They appear around April and
continue through the early summer. This species is
rather slender and elegant, and has a pale beige to
tan cap which may crack slightly when dry. The gills
are adnate and pale buff-brown. The slender stem
has a distinct membranous ring at the top. It grows
in woods, roadsides and open grassy areas
everywhere. Another closely related species is
A. paludosa, which differs in its more slender stature,
preference for damp, marshy places and smaller
spores.

Agrocybe molesta (Lasch) Singer [=*A. dura*]

Cap: 5–7.5cm (2–3in)

Spores: dull, tobacco-brown, 10–14 x 6.5–8μm, smooth

Edibility: edible

The whitish to pale tan cap frequently becomes very cracked with exposure and age. The gills are crowded, adnate and pale buff to brown. The sturdy stem is white, smooth to fibrous and has a narrow ring above. This species, like the previous one, grows principally in spring and prefers open grassy areas or waste places such as roadsides; it is quite common. An *Agrocybe* species that prefers to grow in the autumn is *A. erebia*, and this is easily recognized by its dark, dull brown coloration, and preference for shady woodland paths and hedgerows. The cap colour fades rapidly as it dries out and there is a prominent ring on the stem. It is widespread and common throughout Britain.

Conocybe tenera (Schaeffer) Fayod

Cap: 1–2.5cm (½–1in)

Spores: reddish-brown, 11–12 x 6–7μm, smooth

Edibility: inedible

This is one of a number of difficult-to-distinguish species, but is typical of the group. The bell-shaped cap is smooth, dry and a rich yellow-brown to reddish-brown, fading with age. The narrow gills are almost free and cinnamon-brown. The tall, thin, straight stem is very fragile, pale brown and very finely lined from top to bottom. It is very common in lawns and open grasslands everywhere. The many very similar species in this group are fascinating to study, with many distinctive and beautiful microscopic characters, but they are really the province of the specialist or enthusiastic amateur with access to both microscope and specialist literature.

TRICHOLOMATACEAE
Tricholoma Family

Although the majority of species in this family are white spored, there are some exceptions, of which this is an example. As the spores have a distinct pinkish hue, it is placed here in the guide, with other pink-spored genera, where one might expect to look first.

Rhodotus palmatus (Bulliard ex Fries) Maire
Cap: 2.5–7.5cm (1–3in)
Spores: pink, 6–8μm, globose and warty
Edibility: inedible

A strange but beautiful species, the lovely pink cap has a thick, rubbery-gelatinous cuticle, which is strangely wrinkled and pitted. The stout stem is pink and fibrous, rather tough, and usually set off-centre. A pleasant odour of fruit is present, but the taste is rather bitter, acrid, and unpleasant. It is a rather uncommon species, and grows on deciduous stumps and logs, especially old poplars. The spore print is a distinctly pink to pinkish-ochre. This is the only species in its genus, and its exact relationships to other fungi are unclear, although most mycologists agree it is a member of the giant family Tricholomataceae, albeit a very aberrant one. Other genera in this family that have species with slightly pinkish spores that might be looked for here include *Clitocybe* and *Collybia*.

ENTOLOMATACEAE
Entoloma Family

The Entoloma mushrooms and their relatives all have strange, angular pink spores, or long spores with angular ridges.

Clitopilus prunulus (Scopoli ex Fries) Kummer

Cap: 2.5–7.5cm (1–3in)
Spores: pink, 10–12 x 5–7µm, with longitudinal ridges, appearing angular in end view
Edibility: edible and quite good

Although variable in shape and size, the odour is usually the first clue to identifying this mushroom. It has a strong, almost pungent scent of cucumber or fresh-ground meal. The white cap has the texture of kid leather and starts in-rolled at the margin. The gills are narrow, decurrent, white then pink, while the short stem is often offset from the centre. It can be a very common species and grows on soil in mixed woods everywhere.

Entoloma serrulatum (Persoon) Hesler

Cap: 2.5–5cm (1–2in)
Spores: pink, 7–10 x 5–7.5µm, angular, many-sided
Edibility: inedible

Many *Entoloma* species have beautiful colours, especially blues and violets, and this species has the entire fruit-body coloured deep blue-black to slate-blue. The rounded cap becomes depressed at the centre and is radially fibrous. The gills are very distinctive, being bluish-pink with their edges minutely roughened and deep blue. The stem is slender and smooth. It is quite a common species and grows in grassy areas in woods and pastures. This, and the many other species with an indented and often roughened cap are very often placed into their own genus – *Leptonia* – but many authors (as here) regard them simply as one section of the very large genus *Entoloma*.

Entoloma incanum (Fries) Hesler

Cap: 2–2.5cm (¾–1in)
Spores: pink, 11–14 x 8–9μm, angular, 7–12 sided
Edibility: inedible

An exception to the usual bluish colours in *Entoloma*, this has a bright olive-green to blue-green stem. The cap is olive-green then brownish, finely striate and depressed at the centre. It has the most curious and pungent odour which is usually described as being like mice or burnt hair. Once smelled, it is very specific and unmistakable. It is quite common in open pastureland on chalky soils throughout Britain.

Entoloma sericeum (Bulliard) Quélet

Cap: 2.5–7.5cm (1–3in)
Spores: pink, 7.5–10 x 6.5–8μm, angular
Edibility: inedible

Another species with a strong odour of cucumber or new meal, this mushroom has a fleshy, umbonate to flattened cap which is dark reddish-brown to grey-brown, silky shiny and with the margin noticeably striate. As the cap dries out it becomes much paler. The gills are whitish-grey then pink. The stem is pale brown and fibrous with a white base. The flesh is pale and both smells and tastes mealy. It is a common species in lawns and grasslands everywhere.

Entoloma porphyrophaeum (Fries) Karsten

Cap: 5–10cm (2–4in)
Spores: pink, 10–13 x 6–7μm, angular
Edibility: inedible

One of the largest and certainly one of the tallest species in this country, the domed cap has a soft grey-violet to pinkish-lilac or lilac-brown cap which is finely fibrous. The tall stem is similarly coloured and fibrous with a whitish base. The gills are broad, greyish then pink. It grows in grassy woodland clearings and meadows and is fairly common in the south. A similar, but smaller and darker species, is *E. jubatum*, which is similar in shape. It lacks any lilac or violet tones in the cap, but often has these colours in the gills.

Entoloma clypeatum (Linnaeus) Kummer
Cap: 5–7.5cm (2–3in)
Spores: pink, 8–11 x 7.5–9μm, angular and many-sided
Edibility: inedible

A few species of *Entoloma* grow mainly in the spring and early summer, and this species is fairly common, although often overlooked. It also has a rather unusual choice of habitat, since it grows only under roses, hawthorn and other members of that family. The shield-shaped cap is dull grey-brown, fibrous or streaky, and often cracks at the margin. The gills are sinuate and white then pink. The stout stem is rather short, whitish, tough and fibrous. The flesh has a strong odour and taste of meal or cucumber.

Entoloma lividum Quélet
Cap: 5–12.5cm (2–5in)
Spores: pink, 8–10 x 7–9μm, angular, 5–7 sided
Edibility: poisonous; causes severe gastric upsets and can be quite dangerous

This rather uncommon species is infamous in Europe, where it is referred to as the 'Grand Poisoner'. The large ivory-white to buff cap is umbonate to broadly rounded, smooth to slightly streaky or mottled. The gills are sinuate, crowded and an unusual shade of yellow when young before turning pink. The stout, tough stem is white and fibrous. A strong odour and taste of meal or flour is present. It grows in open, grassy woodlands, especially on chalky soils in the south, but also in the north.

Entoloma nidorosum (Fries) Quélet
Cap: 5–7.5cm (2–3in)
Spores: pink, 7–9 x 6–8μm, angular
Edibility: inedible

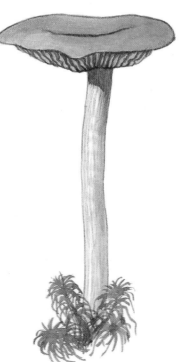

A fairly common odour in a number of unrelated mushrooms is that of bleach or a nitrous smell. In this species it is particularly strong and rather unpleasant. The slightly umbonate then depressed cap is a pale ochre to greyish-yellow, smooth and very hygrophanous as it dries. The gills are broad, whitish-grey, then pink. The tall, slender stem is whitish and striate. It is a common species and prefers wet, almost boggy woodlands under willows or birch, and is widespread in Britain.

PLUTEACEAE
Pluteus Family

These fungi all have gills completely free of the stem and deep salmon-pink spores. One genus (*Volvariella*) has a volva at the base of the stem.

Pluteus cervinus (Schaeffer ex Fries) Kummer
Cap: 5–10cm (2–4in)
Spores: pink, 5.5–7 x 4–5μm, smooth
Edibility: edible but poor quality

One of the commonest of fungi, this can appear at almost any time of year when conditions are suitable. Often when other fungi are scarce in dry weather, fallen logs act as a reservoir of moisture, and this mushroom, along with other *Pluteus* species, will continue to fruit. The cap is very variable in colour, ranging from dull grey-brown to deep chestnut or even pallid, always smooth with fine fibres and some tiny scales at the centre. The broad gills are white, then soon pinkish. The stem is white, fibrous and darker brown below. On the faces of the gills are special bottle-shaped cystidia with 2–3 hook-like projections.

Pluteus petasatus (Fries) Gillet
Cap: 5–15cm (2–6in)
Spores: pink, 6–10 x 4–6μm, smooth
Edibility: edible and good

Looking much like the previous species in overall appearance, this mushroom differs in its white cap with small dark scales at the centre. The gills are usually very broad and rounded at the margin and are very slow to turn pink. The fibrous stem is white and hardly brown below. It is a fairly common species on old deciduous stumps and wood chips, and is widely distributed. It too has large, bottle-like cystidia on the gills with hook-like projections.

Pluteus salicinus (Britzelmayr) Saccardo
Cap: 2.5–5cm (1–2in)
Spores: pink, 6–7 x 5–6μm, smooth
Edibility: doubtful; best avoided

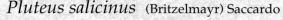

A small, slender species with soft grey-brown to slightly greenish tints in the cap. The gills are whitish then soon pink, while the stem is white with a faint flush of blue-grey or greenish at the base. The cap is usually slightly striate at the margin with age. It is a widespread and common species growing on various fallen trees, especially beech, ash and elm, as well as other species.

Pluteus aurantiorugosus (Trog) Saccardo
Cap: 2.5–5cm (1–2in)
Spores: pink, 5.5–6.5μm, smooth
Edibility: edible

A small but spectacular species, the cap when young is a vivid scarlet but soon fades to bright orange as it expands. This is one of a group of species where the cap cuticle is composed of globose cells rather than the filamentous cells of the previous species. The gills are broad and yellow when young, then soon pinkish. The slender stem is whitish above, yellow-orange below. Sadly, it is rather an uncommon species, found on dead and dying elm trees and maples. It had something of a population explosion during the recent blight of dying elms resulting from Dutch Elm Disease.

Volvariella bombycina (Schaeffer ex Fries) Singer
Cap: 5–15cm (2–6in)
Spores: pink, 6.5–10.5 x 4.5–6.5μm, smooth
Edibility: edible and good

A large and magnificent species, although, sadly, a rare one. The entire mushroom begins enclosed in a thin, egg-like volval sac. This ruptures and the mushroom expands upwards very rapidly. The cap is white to slightly yellowish and beautiful silky-hairy all over. The gills are free, broad and white, then soon pink. The stem is white and fibrous. It grows in clusters, often appearing in old knot-holes and wounds in old elms. Like the previous species, it has been commoner in recent years because of Dutch Elm Disease killing off its host.

Volvariella speciosa (Persoon ex Fries) Singer
Cap: 5–10cm (2–4in)
Spores: pink, 5.5–6.5 x 4–4.5μm, smooth
Edibility: edible

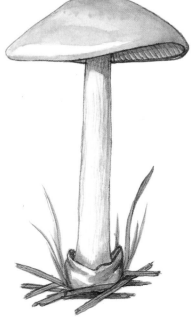

Probably the commonest species in this genus, it grows in old grass in fields, straw heaps or around stables or middens. The silky, whitish-grey cap is often very viscid. The broad gills are white, then soon deep pink. The tall, elegant stem is white, fibrous and emerges from a small, thick volval cup usually buried in the grass. It is a well-known edible species and a very close relative of the Paddy-straw Mushroom popular in Chinese restaurants, but if picking this you must be sure you do not have a poisonous *Amanita* which also has a volva. Remember, *Amanita* has white spores, never pink. It is safer to buy the canned Paddy-straw Mushroom (*V. volvacea*).

ORDER: APHYLLOPHORALES

These fungi all produce spores externally on basidia, but the spore-producing surface is not spread over gills like the gilled mushrooms but on various other surfaces such as wrinkles, spines or fleshy tubes or on simple clubs.

CANTHARELLACEAE
Chanterelle Family

These often delicious edible fungi include the well-known Chanterelle, which is eaten all over the world. They all lack true gills, forming their spores on either a smooth undersurface or on blunt-edged wrinkles or ridges.

> *Craterellus cornucopioides* (Linnaeus ex Fries) Persoon – 'Horn of Plenty'
> **Cap**: 2.5–7.5cm (1–3in)
> **Spores**: white, 10–11 x 6–7μm, smooth
> **Edibility**: edible and delicious; dries well as a spice

This strange fungus also has the rather unfortunate common name in France of Trumpet of Death. This refers to its sombre appearance only, since it is an excellent edible. The thin, black trumpet is hollow all the way down and has a slightly brownish, finely scaly inner surface. The outer surface is black with a finely ridged and wrinkled texture, which becomes whitish with age. It is common, although difficult to spot, and grows in moist, mossy spots, often on stream banks, and can grow in very large numbers.

Pseudocraterellus sinuosus (Fries) Corner

Cap: 2.5–5cm (1–2in)
Spores: ochre, 8–10 x 7–8µm, smooth
Edibility: edible

A rather uncommon species and much paler than the Horn of Plenty shown on page 135. The wavy, irregular trumpets are pale grey-brown and often split. The outer surface is veined and wrinkled and a pale greyish-pink. It has a rather pleasant odour of fruit. It grows on damp, mossy banks and shady areas in both deciduous and coniferous woods.

Cantharellus cibarius Fries – 'Chanterelle'; 'Girolles'

Cap: 2.5–15cm (1–6in)
Spores: pale buff, 8–11 x 4–6µm, smooth
Edibility: edible and delicious

This has almost as many common names as the famous *Boletus edulis*, and almost every country has its own name for it. A delicious edible with a strange fruity flavour, it is collected by the thousand every year all over the world. The yellow-orange caps are thick and fleshy and begin with an in-rolled margin. The undersurface is formed of numerous wrinkled, gill-like ridges, often cross-veined and descending the short stem. The flesh is thick, pale buff and has a wonderful aroma of apricots. It rarely approaches the very large sizes quoted above in Britain, but is a common species under oaks, birch, beech or pine.

Cantharellus tubaeformis Fries

Cap: 2.5–7.5cm (1–3in)
Spores: cream, 8–12 x 6–10µm, smooth
Edibility: edible and good

Not as well known as the Chanterelle, this is nevertheless almost as good an edible and is equally common. It is found in much wetter, boggy situations, usually in *Sphagnum* moss in mixed woods. The thin, trumpet-shaped caps are yellow-brown, while the wrinkled undersurface is yellow then greyish-violet and runs down the stem. The latter is pale yellow to yellow-orange. It is widespread throughout Britain.

Cantharellus cinereus Persoon

Cap: 2.5–7.5cm (1–3in)
Spores: white, 8–10 x 5–7μm, smooth
Edibility: edible and good

One of the rarer species of the Chanterelle family, it is a dark grey-black mushroom, thin-fleshed with a very wrinkled-vein hymenium running down the stem. The stem is short, smooth and grey-black also. Despite its sombre appearance, it has a pleasant fruity odour. Sometimes mistaken for the Horn of Plenty, *Craterellus cornucopioides,* this has an almost smooth hymenium and is completely hollow, and trumpet-like. This species likes damp, mossy woods and is widely distributed. A species that can become black but starts off pale apricot-buff is *C. melanoxeros.* This is very rare (the author has seen it once in some twenty years!), and bruises a dull grey-black colour in all its parts.

Cantharellus lutescens (Persoon) Fries

Cap: 2.5–5cm (1–2in)
Spores: white, 8–10 x 5–7μm, smooth
Edibility: edible and good

Perhaps the rarest species of this group in Britain, it is restricted almost entirely to the Scottish Highlands and grows under pines. The slender fruit-bodies form a hollow trumpet, with the inner surface yellow-orange to yellow-brown and rather scaly at the centre. The hymenium is bright yellow-orange with shallow veins and wrinkles. The stem is smooth and bright yellow. As with most species of *Cantharellus,* the fruit-bodies have a very pleasant, fruity odour, especially when gathered into a basket or bag. These fungi are unusually rich in vitamin A and carotene pigments, more often found in fruits and vegetables than in fungi.

CLAVARIACEAE, RAMARIACEAE AND RELATED FUNGI
Coral and Club Fungi

A large group with a number of smaller families included, as well as those listed above. As their common name suggests, they resemble undersea corals and clubs. Many are among the brightest coloured of fungi and can reach large sizes. Their spores are produced on basidia formed on the outer surface of the clubs.

Ramaria aurea (Fries) Quélet
Cap: 5–15cm (2–6in)
Spores: deep ochre, 8–15 x 3–6µm, roughened
Edibility: edible but not recommended; other
 species cause stomach upsets

A magnificent species. The thick, fleshy, coral-like fruit-body is a bright golden-yellow with masses of tightly packed branches. Each branch ends in a cluster of tiny, cauliflower-like tips. The central stem is paler or almost white. The flesh is white, sometimes marbled, and has a pleasant odour and taste. A rather uncommon species, it can be found in beech woods in the south. The similar species *R. flava* grows under both deciduous and coniferous trees in the north and is usually a little taller, has a more unpleasant odour, and is often slightly bitter to taste.

Ramaria formosa (Fries) Quélet
Cap: 10–20cm (4–8in)
Spores: ochre, 8–15 x 4-6µm, roughened
Edibility: inedible; causes gastric upsets
 and diarrhoea

One of the loveliest of the coral mushrooms, it is also the one which causes the most problems when eaten. Although not deadly, it is a serious purgative and you will certainly regret eating it. The beautiful coral-pink to pinkish-orange branches end in tiny, bright yellow tips. The branches rise from a large, central stem. The flesh is white to pale orange and often bruises wine-pink to purplish-black. A rare species in Britain (rarer now than in the past?), it occurs in beech woods in the south.

Ramaria ochraceovirens (Junghuhn)
Donk [=*R. abietina*]

Cap: 5–10cm (2–4in)
Spores: ochre, 9–10.5 x 3.5–5µm, roughened
Edibility: inedible

A dull-coloured species, it forms a tangle of narrow branches arising from a common stem. The branches are coloured ochre to yellow-olive when young, but as it ages the entire fungus stains olive-green with age or on handling. This is a common species found in the needle litter of pine woods throughout Britain.

Ramaria stricta (Fries) Quélet

Cap: 2.5–10cm (1–4in)
Spores: golden-yellow, 7–10 x 3.5–5.5µm, minutely warted
Edibility: inedible

A distinctive coral fungus in the way the slender branches are held very upright. The branches fork many times but always turn directly upwards and are coloured a dull yellow-brown. All parts bruise darker on handling. The flesh has an unpleasant odour and tastes bitter. It is a fairly common species and grows on conifer logs throughout Britain.

Ramaria botrytis (Fries) Ricken

Cap: 5–15cm (2–6in)
Spores: pale ochre, 11–17 x 4–6µm, with longitudinal lines
Edibility: edible but best avoided; easily confused with poisonous species

This cauliflower-like species has a very broad central stem splitting into numerous smaller branches, each of which are whitish-buff with delicate pinkish-purple tips. The flesh is white, thick and has a pleasant smell. An uncommon species found under beech in the south. Although this is considered a good edible, there are other similar species that cause severe stomach upsets (although they are rarely dangerous), and unless you are absolutely certain of your identification most coral fungi are best left alone.

Pterula multifida (Fries) Fries
Cap: 2.5–7.5cm (1–3in) high
Spores: white, 5–6 x 2.5–3.5μm, smooth
Edibility: inedible

A strange species with extremely slender, densely crowded branches with very fine tips about 1mm (⅟₂₅ in) or less across. There is a central stem at the base and the entire fungus is pale cream to ochre-brown, becoming lilac-brown when old. Unlike most other coral fungi, this has a rather tough, elastic texture. It is an uncommon, although often overlooked, species and grows in needle litter or on wood in conifer woods.

Clavariadelphus fistulosus (Fries) Corner
Cap: 8–30cm (3–12in) high
Spores: white, 10–18 x 5–8μm, smooth
Edibility: edible

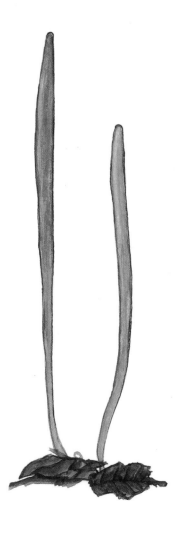

These very slender, elegant clubs are pointed at the tips and are pale ochre-brown in colour and quite smooth. The flesh is whitish and rather brittle. The clubs grow in loose clusters and are found in the leaf litter and woody debris of beech woods and occasionally pine woods and, although widespread, are rather rare. This species is frequently placed in the genus *Macrotyphula*. This comprises a group of closely related species including *M. juncea*, which is even more slender and grows on decomposing stems of herbs and old leaves, and *M. contorta*, which is smaller, more thickset, and often bent and stunted. *M. contorta* grows on dead alders.

Clavariadelphus pistillaris (Fries) Donk
Cap: 7.5–20cm (3–8in) high
Spores: creamy-white, 11–16 x 6–10μm, smooth
Edibility: inedible; rather bitter

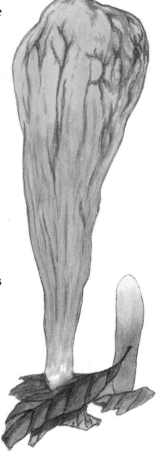

Most people are very surprised when told that this is a fungus, as it is so unlike anything most people consider to be a mushroom or toadstool. The single, large club swells out above and has a wrinkled or furrowed surface when mature. When young it is quite a bright yellow-orange with a paler tip, then slowly turns to ochre-brown or pinkish-brown, often with a lilac tint below. The flesh is white and rather bitter to taste. It grows in small groups standing up out of the leaf litter of beech woods in southern England and is locally common. It also occurs, more rarely, in the Scottish Highlands, where it prefers birch or pine. Some people find this quite palatable, but this would seem to depend on your ability to detect bitter flavours, and whether you find them unpleasant.

Clavariadelphus truncatus (Quélet) Donk

Cap: 5–15cm (2–6in) high

Spores: ochre, 9–13 x 5–8µm, smooth

Edibility: inedible

A much rarer species than the previous one, it is nevertheless quite easy to recognize. The broad clubs are flattened at the top or even slightly depressed, with the sides unevenly wrinkled and ridged. In colour they are pinkish-brown to yellow-ochre. The flesh is white and, unlike the last species, is mild to taste. It grows under conifers in the north.

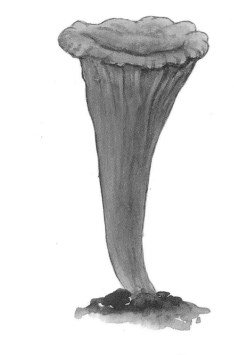

Sparassis crispa (von Wulfen) Fries – 'Cauliflower Mushroom'

Cap: 15–30cm (6–12in) across

Spores: white, 5–7 x 3–5µm, smooth

Edibility: edible and excellent

This remarkable species does indeed look rather like a large cauliflower, or perhaps a cabbage, although much paler in colour. It is formed of numerous flattened, crispy lobes all twisted together to form a ball, and this springs from a tough rooting base or stem buried deep in the ground. The odour is odd – of spice or cheese – and the flavour when cooked is delightfully nutty and crisp. It is a weak parasite of conifers and is usually found at the base of standing trees or near stumps. It is locally common.

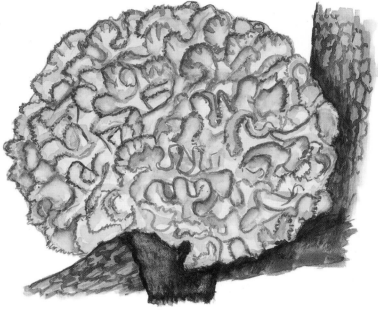

Clavulinopsis fusiformis (Sowerby) Corner

Cap: 5–15cm (2–6in) high

Spores: cream, 5–9 x 4.5–9µm, smooth

Edibility: edible

One of the commonest of the club fungi and also one of the most brightly coloured and easy to identify. The simple, narrow clubs are pointed at the tips and are loosely clustered. Each club is usually hollow in the centre and very brittle. It is common in grasslands and open woods everywhere. Note that the clubs are not truly fused together at a common base but are separate, unlike some other yellow club fungi. This species has also been placed in the genus *Ramariopsis* and the genus *Clavulinopsis* dropped altogether.

Clavaria vermicularis Fries

Cap: 5–15cm (2–6in) high
Spores: white, 5–7 x 3–4μm, smooth
Edibility: edible

The name *vermicularis* means worm-like, and this species does look a little like a cluster of white, wavy worms. The hollow, pointed clubs are very brittle and commonly found in grassy areas and open woodlands. The flesh has a rather earthy smell and taste, and this fungus can hardly be considered as a worthwhile edible. The similar *C. fumosa* differs in its greyish-lilac clubs.

Clavulina cristata (Fries) Schroet

Cap: 2.5–7.5cm (1–3in) across
Spores: white, 7–11 x 6.5–10μm, smooth
Edibility: edible

A common species and, although small, quite attractive. The densely clustered and branched coral is white with finely divided, sharp tips arising from a central stem. The colour can vary to cream or yellowish. The similar *C. cinerea* has greyish branches and usually blunt tips, although once again this varies. Both can be found in mixed woods everywhere. Larger spores (9-13 x 7.5-10μm) and very blunt, irregular dirty-white branches are seen with *C. rugosa*, usually found in conifer woods.

Clavulina amethystina (Fries) Donk

Cap: 2.5–10cm (1–4in) high
Spores: white, 7–12 x 6–8μm, smooth and formed on two-spored basidia
Edibility: edible

Perhaps our loveliest coral fungus, it is unfortunately quite rare, but almost unmistakable. The slender branches are very brittle. They are a bright, clear amethyst, violet or lilac and arise from a central stem. It prefers deciduous woods and seems commoner in the south. The beautiful *Clavaria rosea*, which is rose-pink in colour, differs in its simple, single clubs.

STEREACEAE
Crust Fungi

These form crust-like sheets on wood and occasionally spread out into small shelves or brackets. They do not have tubes on the underside like the true Bracket Fungi (Polypores).

Chondrostereum purpureum (Fries)
Pouzar – 'Silver Leaf Fungus'
Cap: 10–15cm (4–6in) or larger
Spores: white, 5–6.5 x 2–3μm, smooth
Edibility: inedible

This fungus is a common parasite of fruit trees such as apple, plum and cherry, as well as woodland trees, and it cause a characteristic silvery blight on the leaves, hence the common name. It can eventually kill the infected tree. The fungus appears as an irregular crust, which then spreads out to form small brackets and has a lovely lavender-purple edge and undersurface. The top is a dull yellow-ochre to grey-white and hairy or woolly to touch.

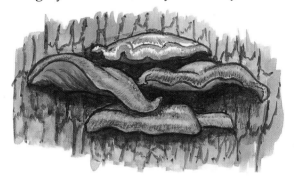

Stereum hirsutum (Willdenow ex Fries)
S. F. Gray
Cap: 1–2.5cm (½–1in) across
Spores: white, 5–8 x 2–3.5μm, smooth
Edibility: tough and inedible

A common species, many individual caps may overlap to form a larger mass and may even fuse together. The upper surface is concentrically zoned in shades of grey, white or brown, and is finely hairy or velvety. The undersurface is smooth and yellow-grey. It grows on fallen timber of birch and beech, as well as other deciduous woods, and is widespread everywhere.

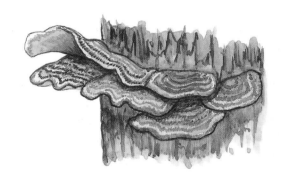

THELEPHORACEAE
Fan Fungi

A group of sombre, fleshy fungi with fan shaped, encrusting or even-stemmed species with dark, spiny spores.

Thelephora terrestris Fries
Cap: 2.5–7.5cm (1–3in)
Spores: purplish-brown, 8–12 x 6–9μm, minutely spiny
Edibility: inedible

Sometimes called the Earth Fan, this does resemble a cluster of dark, feathery fans hugging the soil. The overlapping fans are often rather ragged in outline and are dark blackish-brown to grey-brown. They are tough and fibrous with paler zones. The undersurface is smooth to wrinkled or lumpy. There is usually an earthy or mouldy smell present. It is very common in mixed woods everywhere.

HYDNACEAE AND RELATED FUNGI
Toothed Fungi

These fungi all form their spores on projecting spines or teeth, which usually hang down from the underside of the cap or fruit-body. Some species grow on the ground and have stems, and others form brackets on trees. They are now considered to consist of a number of probably unrelated groups which have evolved independently to use similar spiny structures.

Hydnellum spongiosipes (Peck) Pouzar
Cap: 5–10cm (2–4in)
Spores: brown, 5.5–7 x 5–6μm, warted
Edibility: tough, inedible

This thick, heavy species is remarkable for its very robust, bulbous stem. The cap is irregular, reddish-brown and finely velvety. The short spines on the underside are dark brown and run down the stem. The latter is dark brown and velvety. The flesh is very tough, two-layered with a dark, inner zone. This is an uncommon species which grows in the leaf litter of oak woods and is widely distributed. There are many other species of *Hydnellum*, many with strong tastes and odours and coloured flesh, for example *H. caeruleum*, which has flesh banded with blue and orange and has a mealy odour.

Sarcodon imbricatum (Linnaeus) Karsten
Cap: 10–15cm (4–6in)
Spores: brown, 6–8 x 5–7μm, with large warts
Edibility: inedible

This coarsely scaly species is grey-brown and the rounded cap has the underside densely packed with tiny greyish teeth which run down the stem. The latter is white and more or less central. The flesh is pale brown, soft and tastes rather sharp. An uncommon species, it grows under pines, mostly in Scotland, but also in the south. Other species include *S. scabrosum*, with blackish-green stem base and very bitter taste, and *S. joeides*, with pale lavender flesh which turns green with caustic soda (KOH) solution.

Hydnum repandum Linnaeus
Cap: 5–10cm (2–4in)
Spores: white, 6.5–9 x 6.5–8µm, smooth
Edibility: edible and good

A well-known edible now appearing quite often for sale in specialist food stores. The pale pinkish-orange to orange-buff cap is dry and often irregular in outline. The short spines are pale pinkish-white and descend the short, whitish stem which is usually off-centre. The flesh is white, with a pleasant odour and a spicy or bitter taste. It can grow in large quantities in the leaf litter of beech woods and sometimes conifers throughout Britain.

Hydnum rufescens Fries
Cap: 1–2.5cm (½–1in)
Spores: white, 8–10 x 6–7µm, smooth
Edibility: edible and good

Rather like the previous species, but smaller, with a dark reddish-brown to orange-tawny cap, slightly depressed at the centre. The short spines are whitish-orange, while the slender stem is orange and centrally placed. It prefers pine woods and is regarded as a variety of the previous species by many authorities. Certainly it is possible to find intermediate specimens combining characteristics of both species.

Hericium ramosum (Bulliard ex Mérat)
Letellier [=*H. clathroides*]
Cap: 10–25cm (4–8in) across
Spores: white, 3–5 x 3–4µm, finely roughened
Edibility: edible and delicious

This beautiful species looks rather like an undersea coral growing on a tree and is formed of thin, delicate branches from which hang short (1cm (½ in) or less) spines all the way along each branch. The branches can form much denser masses than illustrated here. The flesh is white and has a crisp, nutty flavour when cooked. It is uncommon to frequent, and grows on old deciduous logs, especially beech, throughout Britain. The similar *H. coralloides* has longer spines, 1–3cm (½–2in), clustered at the ends of the branches, and grows in similar habitats.

Hericium erinaceus (Fries) Persoon
Cap: 10–20cm (4–8in) across
Spores: white, 5–6.5 x 4–5.5μm, minutely roughened
Edibility: edible and delicious

An uncommon but spectacular species, often found growing high up on beech, oak or maple trees. It forms a rounded, compact mass without branches and with hanging spines often several centimetres long. It is widely distributed in Britain and is an excellent edible fungus. Another rare species of toothed fungus on trees is *Creolophus cirrhatus*, which grows on beech. It forms wide, bracket-like fruiting bodies, often in multiple layers, and is white with tiny, densely spiny teeth pointing downwards. It is edible, but considered poor eating.

Auriscalpium vulgare S. F. Gray – 'Earpick Fungus'
Cap: 1–2.5cm (½–1in)
Spores: white, 5–6 x 4–5μm, minutely spiny
Edibility: inedible

The generic name is Latin for 'earpick' and refers to a small instrument used by the Romans for personal hygiene, which resembled this fungus in shape. The small, spoon-shaped fungus has a dark brown, scaly cap with tiny spines on the underside. The thin stem is dark brown and hairy and is attached to one side of the cap. It grows only on fallen and partially rotted pine-cones, and although not uncommon, is easily overlooked in the shady pine woods where it likes to grow. This fungus occurs right across the northern regions of the world, wherever cool pine woods are to be found. It is the only species in its genus and is quite unmistakable.

POLYPORACEAE
Bracket Fungi

All fleshy or woody fungi with their spores produced inside tubes (except for the soft boletes already illustrated) are included here. Many are very large and woody and are common on our woodland trees. Some grow on the ground and can look like a bolete, but are much tougher fleshed. A number are serious parasites of trees.

Polyporus brumalis Fries – 'Winter Polypore'
Cap: 2.5–10cm (1–4in)
Spores: white, 5–7 x 2–2.5μm, sausage-shaped and smooth
Edibility: inedible

One of a group of polypores with a cap and a more or less central, well-formed stem, this species has a smooth yellow-brown to grey-brown cap, whitish tubes with pores spaced 2-3 per millimetre and a slender, grey-brown, minutely hairy stem. It grows on fallen branches, especially of birch, appears from late autumn throughout the winter and into spring, and is very common.

Polyporus varius Fries [=*P. elegans*]
Cap: 5–10cm (2–4in)
Spores: white, 7–10 x 2–3.5μm, sausage-shaped, smooth
Edibility: inedible

A fairly common species, the pale buff cap is smooth and dry and the decurrent tubes are yellowish to pale brown, 4-5 per millimetre. The almost central stem is slender and pale tan with a black lower half. It grows on fallen branches and twigs of deciduous trees. The larger *P. badius* has a shiny, reddish-brown cap and often a completely black stem. Small fruiting bodies of *P. varius* with caps 1-3cm (0.4–1.2in) across are often separated as a variety – var. *nummularius*; this usually has a more circular shape but otherwise hardly seems separable.

Polyporus squamosus Fries – 'Dryad's Saddle'
Cap: 10–30cm (4–12in)
Spores: white, 10–16 x 4–6μm, cylindrical, smooth
Edibility: edible and good when young and tender

Not many polypores are edible but this one is actually very good if found young and if thinly sliced before cooking. The young caps look like strange, blunt knobs growing out of wood, but as they grow the cap expands to often enormous size. The dull, pale ochre cap is marked with bold, flattened, dark brown scales, while the decurrent pores are pale cream, large and honeycomb-like. The short, very tough stem is black at the base. It grows, looking very much like a seat or saddle, out of standing or fallen timber in deciduous woods, and is one of the first fungi to appear in early summer.

Grifola frondosa (Fries) S. F. Gray – 'Hen of the Woods'
Cap: individual caps 2.5–7.5cm (1–3in); entire fruit-body 15–50cm (6–20in)
Spores: white, 5–7 x 3.5–5μm, smooth
Edibility: edible and delicious

Many polypores seem to make use of wounds or injuries in a tree to enter and thus infect it, and some always seem to fruit at the site of an injury. This species commonly fruits at the base of oak trees which have been struck by lightning, and above the site of fruiting can be traced the long, jagged wound caused by the strike. This large species is formed of numerous caps all fused together in one central mass and is a smoky grey-brown above with white tubes and pores below. The flesh is tender when young, then soon tough and fibrous. When young, the soft tips are excellent edibles and highly esteemed in many countries. It is a fairly common species in southern England on oaks and other trees. Much rarer, but in some respects similar, is *Dendropolyporus umbellatus*. This species is also composed of numerous small caps, but each cap is well formed and circular, with central stems, rather than irregular with lateral stems as in *G. frondosa*. Its host tree is usually oak or beech.

Meripilus giganteus (Fries) Karsten
[=*Polyporus giganteus*]

Cap: 25–75cm (10–30in)
Spores: white, 6–7 x 4.5–6μm, smooth
Edibility: edible but rather poor

This is certainly one of the largest fungi you will see in this country and it can hardly be mistaken for anything else. The enormous flattened and wavy caps spring from a lateral base at the bottom of the tree and gradually grow outwards to reach the mature size of nearly 1metre (3ft) across. The dry upper surface is soft and yellow-ochre or tan, while the pores are white; all parts bruise rapidly black on handling. It is a common species in Britain, growing on beech and oak.

Laetiporus sulphureus (Fries) Murrill – 'Chicken Mushroom'

Cap: 10–75cm (4–30in)
Spores: white, 5–7 x 3.5–5μm, smooth
Edibility: edible and delicious when young and tender

The common name originates in North America, where this is one of the most sought-after edible species. It refers to the fact that when cooked the young tips are extremely similar in both taste and texture to chicken. An unmistakable species, it grows on oak, chestnut and occasionally yew, and forms a series of overlapping brackets of a bright yellow-orange colour. In some forms the colour verges on pinkish-orange. It can grow both at the base of trees or very high up and can form masses weighing many pounds. The largest specimen the author has seen required a wheelbarrow to transport it. The fungus causes a serious heart-rot in the trees it infects. Although regarded everywhere as a good edible, there are odd reports of mild upsets from eating this species. In each case it seems to be from eating specimens growing on unusual host trees, such as Eucalyptus or some exotic conifers. It may be that this species absorbs some chemicals from the wood on which it grows. Since finds on exotic trees are very uncommon in Britain, there should be no cause for undue concern.

Postia caesia (Schroeter) Karsten – 'Blue-cheese Polypore' [=*Tyromyces caesius*]

Cap: 5–15cm (2–6in)

Spores: pale blue, 4–5 x 0.7–1µm, sausage-like and smooth

Edibility: inedible

The common name refers to the bluish hue which soon develops over the entire mushroom, especially when it is handled. The squat, rather lumpy bracket is soft and fleshy and has a slightly scurfy or hairy surface and begins a pale greyish-white. The odour is quite fragrant and the taste mild, unlike the similar *P. styptica*, which has a bitter or acrid taste and does not bruise blue. It is a fairly common species in some areas, growing on a variety of dead wood.

Hapalopilus nidulans (Fries) Karsten

Cap: 2.5–12.5cm (1–5in)

Spores: white, 3.5–5 x 2–3µm, smooth

Edibility: inedible

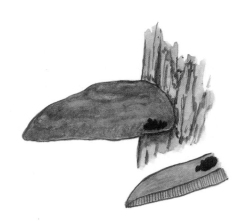

This small bracket is a deep orange-brown, rather fleshy and thick, with small cinnamon-brown pores. The flesh is thick, watery and tawny-brown. A useful chemical test is that all parts turn bright purple-violet with a drop of caustic soda (KOH). It is a common species on fallen logs of deciduous trees throughout Britain.

Piptoporus betulinus (Fries) Karsten – 'Birch Polypore'

Cap: 5–25cm (2–10in)

Spores: white, 5–6 x 1.5µm, sausage-shaped

Edibility: inedible

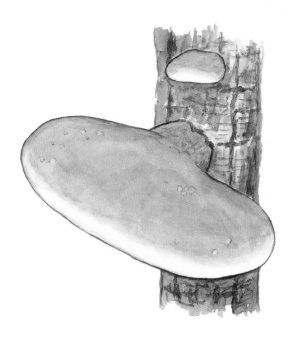

This polypore grows only on birch and can be seen in almost any birch wood the world over. It has been used by man for probably more purposes than almost any other fungus. The soft white flesh makes a good firelighter when dry. It has also been employed to sharpen razors and to halt bleeding as a styptic. Today it is used in museums all over the world, cut into narrow strips, to pin insects in displays. The rounded, kidney-shaped caps are white to pale tan, with a blunt, inrolled margin. A short stem is often present. The white pores are extremely minute.

Trametes versicolor (Fries) Pilat
Cap: 2.5–10cm (1–4in)
Spores: white, 5–6 x 1.5–2.2μm, sausage-shaped
Edibility: inedible

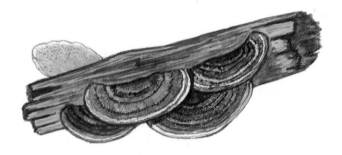

One of the commonest and most well-known bracket fungi, the numerous, overlapping caps can be found in almost any woodland. Each bracket is thin, semicircular and zoned with an amazing variety of colours, from brown to grey, blue-black, yellow or green to purplish. The fine pores are pale yellowish-buff. Old specimens can frequently be seen left over from the previous year.

Daedaliopsis confragosa (Fries) Schroeter
Cap: 5–10cm (2–4in)
Spores: white, 7–11 x 2–3μm, sausage-shaped
Edibility: inedible

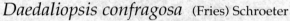

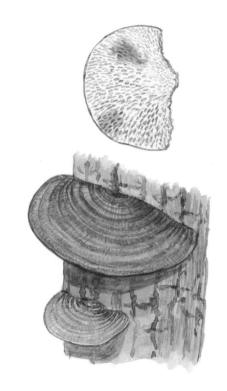

A very common and very variable species with many described forms. The well-formed, semicircular caps are tough and fibrous, grey-brown with numerous paler and darker zones. The pores are very variable and may be round to elongated and maze-like or even gill-like in extreme forms. All will bruise pinkish when handled. It is common on various types of dead wood and may persist for several years.

Daedalea quercina Fries
Cap: 5–15cm (2–6in)
Spores: white, 5.5–7 x 2.5–3.5μm, cylindrical
Edibility: inedible

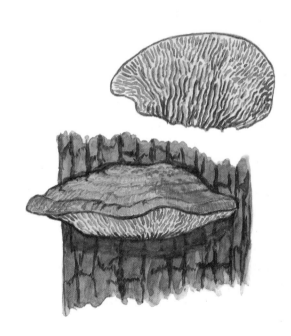

The very thick, tough brackets are smooth to furrowed on top, and a dull white to pale ochre or brown when old. The tubes are extremely thick and elongated to form gill-like plates or strips, and are whitish-buff. It is a common species and grows on dead oak wood throughout Britain. Another species with elongate, gill-like pores is *Lenzites betulina*, which has even narrower, more finely divided pores, is much paler, grey-brown and often greenish from algae, and grows on birch, oak and beech.

Ganoderma applanatum (Persoon ex Wallroth) Patouillard – 'Artist's Fungus'
Cap: 10–50cm (4–20in)
Spores: reddish-brown, 6.5–9.5 x 5–7μm, with a thick, double wall, perforated on the outer layer
Edibility: inedible

This and the closely related *G. adspersum* form large, very hard and woody brackets on dead and dying trees everywhere. The hard upper surface is dry and often lumpy, crust-like and a grey-brown, but often covered with a layer of bright rust-brown spores. The latter are attracted to and held on the surface by a static charge which forms on it. The margin, when actively growing, is white, and the pores on the underside are white, but bruise brown instantly when touched. There may be many layers of tubes since a fresh layer is formed each year and some specimens are many years old. The flesh is pale cinnamon-brown with small whitish flecks. Because of the staining of the pores it is possible to scratch a drawing on the surface and when this dries it is permanent. Museums have specimens with such artwork hundreds of years old. *G. adspersum*, which is much more common, has darker flesh without white flecks, and larger spores 8–13μm long.

Ganoderma lucidum (Curtis ex Fries) Karsten
Cap: 10–25cm (4–10in)
Spores: brown, 7–13 x 6–8μm, ovate with a flattened end
Edibility: inedible, but used to make medicinal teas

Many fungi are being investigated for possible medicinal uses; some are known to be antibiotic in action, others reduce cholesterol, while a few are suspected of having anti-tumour potential for use in cancer treatments. This species is perhaps the most well known of the latter kind. It has been widely researched and studies are still continuing today to find its potential. Many people, particularly in China and the Far East, infuse this and related species in hot water to make a medicinal tea, thought to have restorative properties. The beautiful brackets have a highly polished, lacquered appearance and vary from chestnut to reddish-purple or almost black. A distinct lateral stem is often present. The growing margin and the tubes are whitish-buff. It is a fairly common species on oaks, chestnut and some other trees in the south.

Fistulina hepatica Schaeffer ex Fries –
'Beefsteak Polypore'; 'Ox Tongue'
>   **Cap**: 7.5–25cm (3–10in)
>   **Spores**: pinkish-salmon, 4.5–6 x 3–4µm, smooth
>   **Edibility**: edible, but an acquired taste

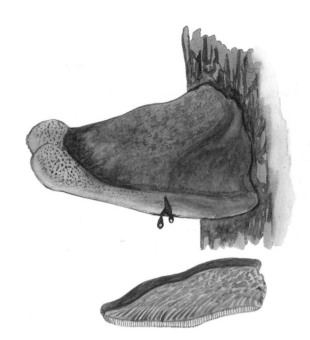

A strange fungus, it really does look like the tongue of an animal and feels like one too. The soft, reddish bracket is spongy and moist on the upper surface, and usually minutely pimpled and roughened. It may be very viscid when wet. The tubes are pale reddish, while the pores are cream, and the tubes are very easily separated from each other. The flesh is fibrous and very moist, dripping a reddish-brown liquid when cut. The taste is rather acidic, and although some people like to eat it, most consider it rather too unusual. It is a common fungus on old oak trees and occasionally on chestnut, and is widespread.

Fomes fomentarius (Linnaeus ex Fries) Fries
>   **Cap**: 5–20cm (2–8in)
>   **Spores**: yellowish, 15–20 x 5–7µm
>   **Edibility**: inedible

Forming hard, hoof-shaped brackets, it has a concentrically grooved crust coloured grey-brown to yellow-brown or even blackish. The pores are white to dull brownish and bruise slightly darker. The flesh is woody and cinnamon-brown with an acrid taste. It is commonest in the north, where it grows on birch, but it can be found in the south, where it grows on beech and sycamore.

Schizophyllum commune Fries
>   **Cap**: 1–5cm (½–2in)
>   **Spores**: white, 3–4 x 1–2.5µm
>   **Edibility**: inedible

At first sight this might look like a gilled mushroom but a closer look will show that the 'gills' are very strange, split down the middle and often curled over lengthwise. It is, in fact, closely related to the polypores, and the 'gills' are similar to very elongated tubes. The cap surface is white and very hairy and the margin is usually lobed. It grows in large numbers on a wide variety of woods the world over and can survive droughts by rolling up until wet weather returns.

Although this is now considered by most mycologists to be a rather artificial grouping of fungi which are not really closely related, it is nevertheless a very convenient one for use in guide books, since it brings together all those fungi which produce their spores inside the fruit-body, rather than on an external hymenium. The spores in Gasteromycetes are not forcefully ejected by the basidium so they rely to a great extent on external forces – wind, rain and insects – to carry off their spores, and have evolved some of the strangest forms to accomplish this.

ORDER: PHALLALES

Fungi with the spore-mass (gleba) contained in an 'egg' and frequently expanding rapidly to produce strange-shaped fruit-bodies. The spore mass then liquefies and gives off an unpleasant odour to attract insects, which eat the spores and unknowingly pass them on to germinate elsewhere.

PHALLACEAE
Stinkhorn Family

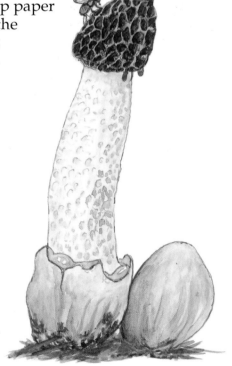

The stinkhorns can be 'hatched' by placing the unopen eggs on a damp paper towel under a glass. The strange, phallic shapes and foul odours are the source of various folktales usually connected with witches and black magic; other tales relate that they grow where rutting deer have been, while in the Far East they are regarded as aphrodisiacs.

Phallus hadriani Venturi
   Cap: 10–15cm (4–6in) high
   Spores: 4–5 x 2µm
   Edibility: only when young

This has the typical stinkhorn structure of a spongy stem emerging from an egg; in this instance the egg is tinted a purplish-pink. At the top of the stem is a ridged and pitted, thimble-like cap over which is spread the olive spore-mass. Shortly after emerging, the spore mass will liquefy and release the powerful odour; in this species it has a rather sweet component like hyacinths mixed with rotting vegetables. A rare species in Britain, it is confined to sandy coastal areas, often in the slacks behind sand-dunes.

Phallus impudicus Linnaeus – 'Stinkhorn'

Cap: 10–15cm (4–6in) high

Spores: 4–5 x 2µm

Edibility: the eggs are a delicacy when unopened

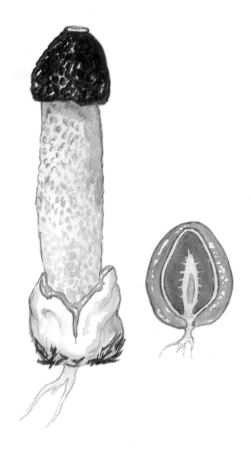

Many people are aware of this species by its putrid odour but never realize that it is caused by a fungus, usually suspecting a dead animal or perhaps the sewage system. Starting as a white egg, it soon splits and out pushes a spongy white stem on which is perched a ridged and pitted cap. On the cap is spread the olive-green spore-mass and this soon liquefies to release the powerful, fetid odour which attracts flies and slugs from a great distance. The eggs have tough white mycelial cords at the base, and these have been traced through a woodland, moving from stump to stump, often for many hundreds of yards, infecting dozens of old stumps throughout the woodland. A very common species everywhere.

Mutinus caninus (Hudson) Fries

Cap: 7.5–12.5cm (3–5in high)

Spores: 3–4 x 1.5µm

Edibility: inedible

A slender, delicate species and much less odorous than other stinkhorns; indeed, you may hardly smell it at all.The slender stem emerges from a small white egg and is white to pale orange with a narrow apex which is coloured bright red or orange. Over this apex is the dark olive spore-mass which liquifies shortly after emergence. Note that there is no separate cap as in the previous two species. A fairly common species, it grows in clusters, usually in beech woods. This is a genus of fungi that is much more common and with many more species in the tropics and in North America. As is usual with all the phalloid fungi, the tropical species are often much more grotesque, brightly coloured and with a more fetid odour. All these characteristics are aimed at attracting insects and other invertebrates, which will eat, and subsequently disperse the spores.

CLATHRACEAE
Cage Stinkhorn Family

Related to the Common Stinkhorns, these fungi resemble
cages or baskets, or sometimes squids with tentacles.
Like other Stinkhorns, they 'hatch' from an egg.

Clathrus ruber Micheli ex Persoon – 'Cage
Stinkhorn'; 'Lattice Stinkhorn'
> **Cap**: 5–15cm (2–6in)
> **Spores**: 5–6 x 1.5–2.5μm
> **Edibility**: inedible

A rare prize in Britain, where it was probably introduced but is now naturalized.
Unmistakable, it forms a large, spongy, cage-like structure which erupts out of a white egg.
The inner surface of the cage is smeared with the gleba, which liquefies and gives off the
strong, fetid odour. It is found in a few scattered localities in gardens and shrubberies in the
south of England and the Isle of Wight, but is common in southern Europe. Another name for
this fungus is *Clathrus cancellatus*. Historically, this species has been much disliked or even
feared in country districts of Europe, and was thought to produce skin complaints if touched,
or sickness if the odour was inhaled. None of these fears seem to have any basis in reality.
What is certain, however, is that the odour is so strong and unpleasant that it makes painting
its portrait very difficult!

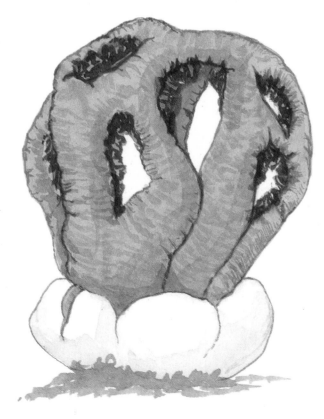

ORDER: LYCOPERDALES

This large Order includes the familiar Puffballs, and Earthstars, which all produce their spore-mass (gleba) inside a ball-like structure (peridium).

LYCOPERDACEAE
Puffball Family

As their common name suggests, members of this family are ball-like, and the spores inside the ball become dry and powdery and will puff out if the ball is tapped.

Vascellum pratense (Persoon) Kreisel
Fruit-body: 2.5–5cm (1–2in)

Spores: olive, 3–5.5μm, globose and finely warted

Edibility: edible when young

Common everywhere on lawns, fields and golf courses, this and other species can be the bane of the golfer, who mistakes it for a ball. The small whitish to yellowish ball has a scurfy, powdery covering of tiny spines which easily rub off. The base of the ball has a short, sterile stem. The gleba starts white but soon matures to a dark olive-brown.

Lycoperdon echinatum Persoon ex Fries
Fruit-body: 2.5–5cm (1–2in)

Spores: brown, 4–6μm, globose and warty

Edibility: edible when young

This pale brown puffball is remarkable for the coating of very long, pointed spines. These are in groups with their tips touching and can be almost 5mm (¼in) long. They will rub off to leave a dark network pattern on the cuticle. The spore-mass or gleba matures to a dark purplish-brown and emerges through an opening at the top. Rather uncommon, it grows in deciduous woods, especially beech, throughout Britain.

Lycoperdon mammiforme Persoon
Fruit-body: 5–7.5cm (2–3in)

Spores: brown, 4–5μm, globose and warted

Edibility: edible when young

This species is unusual for the way in which the outer wall breaks up to form numerous woolly patches and scales and leaves a ring-like zone around the base. The spore-mass is dark purple-brown when mature. It is a rare species of woodlands on chalky soils.

Lycoperdon pyriforme Schaeffer ex Persoon
Fruit-body: 2–4.5cm (⅝–1¾in)
Spores: olive-brown, 3–4.5μm, globose, smooth
Edibility: edible when young

Growing in large clusters, this is a common sight on old stumps. The pear-shaped puffballs are white to dull buff when old and are attached to the wood by thick, white mycelial strands. The skin has a fine, scurfy-granular coating when young but is soon smooth. The spores begin white then mature to olive-brown. It is widespread everywhere.

Lycoperdon foetidum Bonord
Fruit-body: 2.5–5cm (1–2in)
Spores: dull brown, 4–5μm, globose and minutely spiny
Edibility: edible when young

This species has tiny, dark brown spines, even when young. The puffball is whitish-buff when young, then matures to a dull yellow-brown with darker, blackish-brown spines. The spore mass is a dull sepia-brown and has a strong, unpleasant odour (several other species also develop strong odours with age). It is a common species, especially under conifers, and is widely distributed.

Lycoperdon perlatum Persoon
Fruit-body: 2.5–5cm (1–2in)
Spores: olive-ochre, 3.5–4.5 μm, globose and minutely warted
Edibility: edible when young

An extremely common species, the rounded to slightly club-shaped ball has small white spines or warts, often in tiny rings which are easily rubbed off, leaving round marks. A short, well-developed sterile base is present. It grows in fields, roadsides and gardens, as well as grassy clearings in woods, and is widely distributed.

Calvatia excipuliformis (Persoon) Perdek
Fruit-body: 7.5–15cm (3–6in) high
Spores: olive-brown, 3.5–5.5μm, warted
Edibility: edible when young

This can form a very large, club-shaped fruit-body with a long, well-developed sterile base. The white cuticle is finely roughened or granular with small warts which rub off with age. The white gleba slowly matures to dark olive-brown. Eventually the ball will break down to release the spores, and only the sterile base may be left behind. It is a common species in woods everywhere.

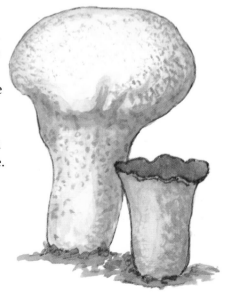

Calvatia utriformis (Bulliard ex Persoon) Jaap
Fruit-body: 7.5–12.5cm (3–5in)
Spores: olive, 4–5μm, warted
Edibility: edible when young

A large, squat species without the tall sterile base of the previous species. The white to pale brown skin has a layer of cottony, scurfy warts which soon break up and fall off. Gradually the entire outer wall of the puffball breaks apart and the spores are released. Often all that is left some months later is the short sterile base. It is a common species of heathlands and fields, especially in the north.

Bovista plumbea Persoon ex Fries
Fruit-body: 2–3cm (⅘–1in)
Spores: olive, 4.5–6μm, globose with a very long pedicel or stalk
Edibility: edible when young

Looking like a small golf ball when young and fresh, the outer white skin soon flakes away to expose a lead-grey inner surface. This encloses the olive-brown spore-mass. It is quite common and prefers short grass in pastures and lawns.

Langermannia gigantea (Batsch)
Rotskovius – 'Giant Puffball' [=*Calvatia gigantea*]
Fruit-body: 20–50cm (8–20in) across
Spores: yellow-brown, 3.5–5.5μm, minutely warted
Edibility: edible and good when young and still white

One of the monsters of the fungus world, giant specimens are said to have been mistaken for sheep. The rather long, flattened ball is white with a matt, suede-like skin which slowly erodes away to expose the yellow-brown mature spore-mass. When young and the gleba is still white and firm, the fungus can be sliced and cooked and is an excellent edible. This is one of those species that has distinct flushes in some years and then is subsequently very scarce. When fruiting well it may appear by the hundred and likes banks and hedgerows, woodland edges and gardens, as well as fields.

GEASTRACEAE
Earthstar Family

These remarkable fungi have a strangely animal-like appearance with their star-shaped arms lifting them off the leaf litter. The spores are either sucked out by wind, blowing over the opening in the inner ball, or by raindrops hitting the inner wall and so puffing them out. In some species the arms can repeatedly open and close, depending on the weather.

Geastrum triplex Junghuhn – 'Earthstar'
Fruit-body: 2.5–10cm (1–4in)
Spores: dark brown, 3.5–4.5μm, globose and warted
Edibility: inedible

When young and unopened they look just like a bunch of dark brown onions lying in the leaf litter. Slowly the thick, leathery outer layer (peridium) splits to form a number of fleshy arms, which curve backwards to reveal the inner ball containing the gleba. Surrounding the pale brown ball is a distinct, irregular collar. The spores are released by the action of wind and raindrops via a tiny apical hole in the ball. This is a common species in beech woods throughout Britain.

Geastrum pectinatum Persoon
Fruit-body: 2.5–5cm (1–2in)
Spores: brown, 4–6μm, globose and warted
Edibility: inedible

The small, tough, grey-brown ball splits to form a star, and at the centre is a rounded grey-white ball set on a slender stalk. The ball has a narrow, beaked and deeply grooved opening at the top from which the spores are released. This species grows in woods and gardens, especially near cedars, and is widespread but rather uncommon. There are many other species, some frequent and some quite rare. Among the commoner species are *G. sessile*, where the spore sac sits directly on the open arms without any collar or stem; and *G. bryanti*, a tiny (3-4cm [1.2–1.6in] across) species, with a stalked spore sac and a long, pointed opening (peristome) with a circular, grooved base.

ORDER: SCLERODERMATALES

Fungi related by their lack of a true sterile base, (common in the puffballs), spore mass without sterile, thread-like cells (capillitium) and spores colouring before they turn powdery.

ASTRAEACEAE
False Earthstar Family

Resembling Earthstars, these are in fact closely related to the Earthballs, (*Scleroderma*) with similar ornamented, dark spores.

Astraeus hygrometricus (Persoon) Morgan
  Fruit-body: 2.5–5cm (1–2in)
  Spores: brown, 7–11μm, warted
  Edibility: inedible

An unusual species, and something of a weather indicator. After the arms have split apart they will remain open if the weather is moist. If the weather turns dry, the arms will reclose to reduce evaporation. The arms have an irregularly cracked and warty surface, while the ball is pale brown and smooth with a small apical spore. It is a rare species in Britain, found in sandy soils, often buried in the soil and then pushing up as it expands. Although it looks very much like a normal Earthstar, it is much more closely related to the Earthballs described below.

SCLERODERMATACEAE
Earthball Family

The Earthballs resemble Puffballs in some respects but their outer wall (peridium) is much tougher and leathery, and often warty. The spores are coloured and usually spiny or warty to reticulate. Most species are poisonous if eaten in any quantity.

☠

Scleroderma citrinum Persoon – 'Common Earthball'
  Fruit-body: 5–10cm (2–4in)
  Spores: purple-black, 8–12μm, globose with tall
   spines and an indistinct network
  Edibility: poisonous

One of the most abundant fungi in summer and autumn, this species has a very thick outer wall (peridium), which is tawny-yellow, and has fine to very coarse warts. The gleba starts white but rapidly turns purple-black with odd mottlings and whitish streaks. There is a strong, pungent odour, very distinctive but difficult to define, rather rubber-like perhaps. It grows in mixed deciduous woods everywhere. *S. bovista* is smaller, smoother and has spores with a very distinct network below the spines.

Scleroderma verrucosum (Bulliard)

Persoon – 'Stalked Earthball'

Fruit-body: 2.5–7.5cm (1–3in)

Spores: olive-brown, 10–14μm, globose with small, sharp spines

Edibility: poisonous

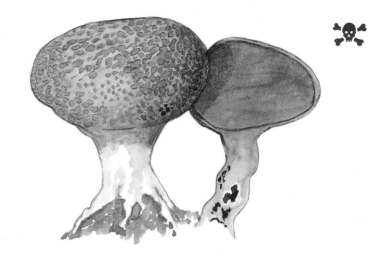

The long stalk with prominent mycelial roots binding together the soil is the first clue in identifying this species. Next is the rather smooth peridium with only tiny warts and the rather thin peridial wall. Finally, the spiny spores will confirm the identification. It is not uncommon in some areas and prefers sandy or light, chalky soils. The closely related *S. areolatum* is often more commonly found in some areas, and is best distinguished by its larger spores (11-13μm across) and usually smaller rooting base. The tiny warts on the skin of the earthball are often surrounded by a circle or areola, hence the specific name.

Pisolithus tinctorius (Persoon)

Coker & Couch – 'Dye-maker's Mushroom'

Fruit-body: 5–10cm (2–4in) across, 5–20cm (2–8in) high.

Spores: brown, 7-12μm, spiny

Edibility: inedible

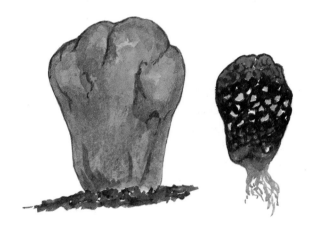

This rather ugly mushroom begins life buried in the soil with a deeply rooting, tough mycelial base, and then slowly pushes up out of the soil. The outer skin is ochre to reddish-brown and very irregular in shape, while the spore-mass consists of small whitish to yellow balls like small peas embedded in a blackish jelly. This eventually breaks down into a brown spore powder. Despite its ugly appearance, it is highly prized for its use in dyeing. When boiled down it gives a rich golden-brown to blackish dye. It is a rare species in this country, known only in a few sandy pine woods in southern England. It also occurs in dry soils all over the world. This species forms a mycorrhizal association with several tree species, and is currently being used in several reforestation projects to encourage tree growth.

ORDER: TULOSTOMATALES

Sometimes called the stalked puffballs, these have the most well-developed stems and often bizarre forms of any of the puffball-type fungi. There are about six genera, of which only two are at all common in Britain.

TULOSTOMATACEAE
Stalked Puffball Family

Resembling a tiny puffball on a long, slender stem.

Tulostoma brumale Persoon
Fruit-body: about 2cm (¾in) across, stem about 4cm (1½in) high
Spores: brown, 3-5µm, globose, minutely warted
Edibility: inedible

A strange, inconspicuous species only rarely reported. It prefers dry, sandy soils and has even been found in old, drystone walls in towns. The small puffball is a pale whitish-grey and is seated on a slender white stem with a bulbous base, which is often buried in the soil. It is locally common but a keen eye is needed to spot one.

Battareae phalloides (Dickson) Persoon
Fruit-body: 15–25cm (6–10in) high
Spores: brown, 5-5.5 x 6.0µm, subglobose
Edibility: inedible

An extremely rare and fascinating fungus, this is like no other species you will come across in Britain, although other species of *Battareae* occur in other parts of the world. It is essentially like a puffball or earthball raised up on a long, shaggy stalk, and this emerges from a volva buried in the sandy soil it prefers. The rusty-brown spores are contained in the ball-like cap, which breaks down slowly and releases them by the action of wind and rain. The entire fungus begins enclosed in the volva, but rapidly elongates upwards to lift the spore mass into the open air. It grows in sandy banks and hedgerows, and even inside hollow trees where loose soil has accumulated. It is widespread but very rare in southern England, more often reported in the warmer parts of continental Europe.

ORDER: NIDULARIALES

A group of about four genera in two families, all with the common character of tiny egg-like spore masses (peridioles) contained in a cup or nest, and relying on mechanical means (raindrops or a flexing of the cup wall) to propel the eggs out of the cup.

NIDULARIACEAE
Bird's Nest Fungi

The most nest-like fungi of the order, with three genera, of which *Nidularia* is rather rare and not shown here; it forms a globular structure with a thin, simple wall that splits irregularly to reveal its peridioles.

Cyathus striatus (Hudson) Willdenow – 'Bird's Nest Fungus'
Fruit-body: 0.6–2cm (¼–⅜in)
Spores: 15–20 x 8–12µm, smooth
Edibility: inedible

The urn- or vase-shaped nests are brown and hairy on the outside but smooth and silvery-grey on the inside, which is distinctly lined and grooved. At the bottom are tiny dark eggs attached by coiled cords waiting to be splashed out by raindrops. This is a locally common species and grows in woodlands on fallen twigs and branches.

Cyathus olla (Batsch) Persoon
Fruit-body: 0.6–1cm (¼–⅜in)
Spores: 11–13 x 7–8µm, smooth
Edibility: inedible

The tiny, flared funnel-like nests of this species are brown and slightly roughened on the outside. The inner surface is smooth and white to pale grey. The eggs are whitish-grey. This species prefers more open, arable land and is common in fields and pastures, as well as on sand-dunes, and on woody debris, and is widely distributed.

Crucibulum laeve (Hudson) Kambly

Fruit-body: 0.6–1cm (¼–⅜in)

Spores: 4–10 x 4–6µm, smooth

Edibility: inedible

The almost cylindrical nests are tawny-yellow and begin with a hairy lid covering the opening. This splits open to reveal the smooth inner surface and the creamy-yellow, lens-shaped peridioles or eggs inside. It grows on dead wood and woody debris and is widespread in Britain.

SPHAEROBOLACEAE
Catapult or cannon fungi

A unique family, with just one genus and species. It is quite unmistakable, but easily overlooked because of its tiny size. It is considered to be related to the other bird's nest fungi, although differing in its method of spore dispersal.

Sphaerobolus stellatus Tode

Fruit-body: 1.5–2.5mm (½₂–³⁄₃₂in) across

Spores: white, 7.5–10 x 4–5.5µm

Edibility: inedible

Although only just qualifying as a larger fungus (it really needs the use of a hand-lens), it is included here because of its remarkable method of spore dispersal. It is a unique example of a fungal catapult. The tiny whitish balls split open to form a yellowish star with a single brownish ball of spores at the centre. The inner layer of the star suddenly flips outwards, thus propelling the egg into the air. Eggs have been recorded travelling up to 4m (13ft) – this is equivalent to a human throwing a discus about one mile (1.6 kilometres)! The fungus appears to need at least some light to stimulate the catapult action, since spore dispersal ceases in complete darkness. This is a common, if rarely seen, species and grows on sawdust, dung and other organic debris.

ORDER: TREMELLALES

These fungi belong to a large group which share the common feature of having their spore-producing cells – the basidia – divided (septate) either longitudinally or transversely. They usually have a jelly-like or rubbery consistency.

AURICULARIACEAE
Tree Ear fungi

A relatively small family, with only a few genera and species world-wide. They all have a more or less rubbery consistency, and rather membranous forms. One species, *Auricularia polytricha*, is widely cultivated in the Far East for food, particularly in China.

Auricularia auricula-judae (Bulliard ex St Amans) Berkeley – 'Tree Ear'; 'Jew's Ear'
  Fruit-body: 2.5–15cm (1–6in)
  Spores: white, 12–15 x 4–6μm, sausage-like
  Edibility: edible; considered a delicacy

A strange fungus with an interesting folklore attached. The first common name is obvious, as it does indeed resemble an ear. The second name is a corruption of Judas's Ear and refers to the legend that Judas Iscariot hanged himself on an elder tree, one of the favourite hosts of this fungus. It is supposed to be his spirit appearing as this strange, ear-like form. The dark, purple-brown ears are rubbery in texture and slightly velvety on the outside. It is common everywhere and grows on a wide range of host trees. The basidia are divided transversely. A similar oriental species is widely esteemed as an edible and is commonly served in Chinese restaurants.

TREMELLACEAE
Jelly Fungus Family (part)

Very variable in shape, from shapeless jelly to
rounded or tongue-shaped or even trumpet-shaped,
all species have basidia longitudinally septate.

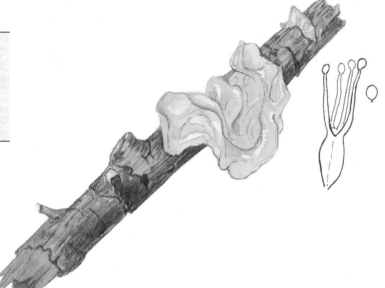

Tremella mesenterica Retz ex Fries –
'Witches' Butter'
> **Fruit-body**: 2.5–10cm (1–4in)
> **Spores**: yellowish, 7–15 x 6–10μm, smooth
> **Edibility**: inedible

The commonest jelly fungus that most people find,
this species varies from a bright yellow to almost
white or transparent. It forms irregular lobes and
wrinkled masses and grows from fallen branches
and twigs at almost any time of the year when the
weather is damp. When the weather turns dry the
fungus shrinks and becomes a shrivelled, hard
lump, only to revive again when it rains.

Tremiscus helvelloides (Persoon) Donk
[=*Phlogiotis helvelloides*]
> **Fruit-body**: 2.5–10cm (1–4in)
> **Spores**: white, 9–12 x 4–6μm
> **Edibility**: edible and considered a delicacy,
> although rather tasteless; in any case, it is too
> rare and should not be disturbed

A wonderful species and one which is happily
spreading in this country although still a rarity. The
beautiful funnel-shaped, lobed and wavy fruit-
bodies are a clear pink to apricot and quite
unmistakable. The flesh is soft and rubbery. The
basidia are longitudinally septate. It grows in large
groups on the ground below conifers, with a
scattered but wide distribution. Whether this is a
natural part of the British flora, which is only now
making a sudden expansion of its territory, or
whether it is an introduced species from mainland
Europe is as yet uncertain.

DACRYMYCETACEAE
Jelly Fungus Family (part)

Gelatinous, rounded to club-like fungi with long, narrow, horn-like two-spored basidia.

Calocera viscosa (Persoon ex Fries) Fries
Fruit-body: 2.5–10cm (1–4in)
Spores: ochre-yellow, 9–14 x 3–5µm, sausage-shaped
Edibility: inedible

At first sight this looks very like a coral or club fungus, but if you feel it, the texture is distinctly rubbery and gelatinous, not brittle like a typical club fungus. The bright yellow-orange branches split into smaller points. When dry it may shrivel into a small, dark orange, hard lump. The basidia are shaped very much like a tuning fork. It is very common on dead coniferous wood everywhere. The smaller *C. cornea* differs in its single, unforked branches and grows on deciduous woods.

Calocera cornea (Batsch ex Fries) Fries
Fruit-body: 5–10cm (⅕–⅖in) high
Spores: cylindric-elliptic, 7–10 x 2.5–5µm
Edibility: inedible

This tiny species may be found in enormous numbers spread out over the surface of fallen logs, especially oak and beech. The clubs are usually simple, although occasionally they will fork, and are soft and gelatinous, or rubbery when moist. When dry, however, they shrivel to tiny, hard, bony spikes of a much darker orange. As soon as a shower of rain occurs and the air is humid again they swell and resume their normal shape, and begin to produce spores as if nothing had happened. The species is widespread throughout the northern hemisphere.

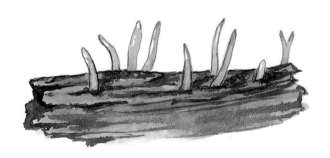

CLASS ASCOMYCETES

These fungi produce their spores in quite a different way from all the other fungi shown in this book. Their spores are produced in long cells called asci, usually eight spores per ascus, although this can vary from genus to genus. The spores are ejected from the cell like bullets from a gun, often producing a cloud of spores above the fungus which you can both see and hear when you pick or disturb it. The asci give the entire group its name – the Ascomycetes. This is an enormous group of fungi with many thousands of species, mostly small and dealt with only in specialist literature. But it does also include such large and well-known edibles as the Morels, as well as some very poisonous species such as the False Morels.

Morchella esculenta Linnaeus ex Fries –
'Common Morel'; 'Yellow Morel'
> **Fruit-body**: 5–12.5cm (2–5in) high
> **Spores**: deep yellow-ochre, 20–24 x 12–24μm, smooth
> **Edibility**: edible and excellent, one of the best

Part of the attraction in hunting for these fungi is the challenge of finding them. They are elusive and fruit for only a short time in the spring. They are very fussy about where they will fruit, preferring the ground around dying apple trees, elms and ash on chalky soils. The cap begins as a tightly compressed greyish sponge with lighter ridges, and expands to form a large, yellowish sponge with large pits and ridges raised on a large white stem. The entire fungus is hollow (wonderful stuffed and baked!) with a swollen base. The microscopic asci with their spores line the pits and ridges. It begins fruiting around the end of April and finishes around the end of May.

Morchella elata Fries – 'Black Morel'
> **Fruit-body**: 5–12.5cm (2–5in) high
> **Spores**: pale ochre, 24–28 x 12–14μm, smooth
> **Edibility**: edible and excellent

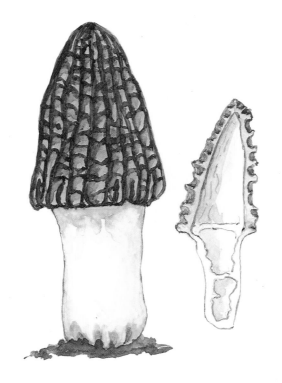

The cap of this species is tall and rather conical with narrow, more or less vertical ridges connected by cross-ridges. The colour is dark brown to smoky grey-black with darker ridges. The stem is white and cylindrical. This species seems to prefer conifers or ash trees but more details are needed as to habitat preferences. Like the previous species it grows only in the spring. There is great variation in the shape and colours of morels, and numerous species have been described. However, as yet, there is little agreement as to how to define them. Closer attention to spore colour (rarely mentioned for morels), and examination of the spores via electron scan microscopy (which allows ultra high magnification of surface detail) shows promise of providing answers to this difficult problem.

Morchella hortensis Boudier
Fruit-body: 5–10cm (2–4in)
Spores: pale yellow, 19–22 x 15–16μm, smooth
Edibility: edible and excellent

A rare and little-known species, it seems to like more urban, disturbed habitats and frequently appears in flowerpots in greenhouses and in gardens. The dark, blackish-brown cap has noticeably parallel ridges, but unlike the previous species, the cap is oval and often curiously flattened. Where it meets the stem there is almost no overhang or depression. Like other Morels it is edible and very good.

Morchella conica (Persoon) Boudier
Fruit-body: 5–7.5cm (2–3in) high
Spores: medium yellow, 20–25 x 15–17μm, smooth
Edibility: edible and excellent

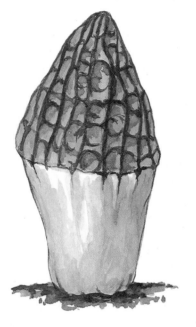

This is a much-disputed species, with some authorities placing it as a form of *M. elata*. However, the author has found collections which seemed distinct and agreed well with Boudier's description, so it is included here in the hope that it will stimulate further investigation and records. The short, very conical cap has parallel ridges with cross-connectives and is dark brown with blackish ridges. The very short stem joins the stem with almost no division or overhang of the cap, unlike *M. elata*. It is a rare species of open, chalky grasslands near shrubs in the south of England.

Verpa conica Swartz ex Persoon
Fruit-body: 2.5–10cm (1–4in) high
Spores: pale ochre, 22–26 x 12–16μm, smooth
Edibility: edible but not very choice

This looks exactly like a small thimble raised on a cylindrical, roughened stem. The 'thimble' is pale brown and smooth, attached only by its very apex to the white, granular stem. It is an uncommon but easily overlooked species, preferring dense, shady woodlands and old orchards. It is quite widespread.

Mitrophora semilibera A. P. de Candolle ex Fries

Fruit-body: 2.5–12.5cm (1–5in) high
Spores: pale ochre, 24–30 x 12–15µm, smooth
Edibility: edible but not as good as other Morels

This species varies greatly in the proportion of the stem compared to the cap. Some specimens have long, swollen stems like a Stinkhorn, while others have a stem no larger than the cap. The latter is conical with blunt, parallel ridges and is brown. The fragile, thin-fleshed stem is white with a granular surface and completely hollow. It appears a week or so earlier than the other Morels, and grows under mixed trees on chalky soils. This is placed in the genus *Mitrophora* because of the half-free cap attachment, but this is really a very poor character on which to separate a genus, so many authors, including this one, would prefer to place it with the other morels in *Morchella*, at which time the older name, *Morchella hybrida*, would take precedence.

Helvella crispa Scopoli ex Fries

Fruit-body: 2.5–10cm (1–4in) high
Spores: cream, 18–21 x 10–13µm, smooth
Edibility: edibility uncertain, best avoided

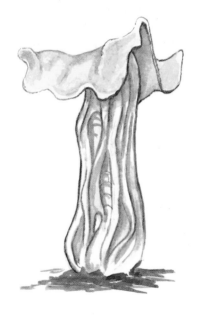

A lovely species with a white to cream, saddle-shaped cap raised up on a strange fluted white stem. The flesh is thin and very fragile, and the fungus is hollow with several convoluted chambers. It grows in the autumn and is widespread in mixed woodlands everywhere. Although usually regarded as a reasonably good edible, there is enough doubt about the entire group of false morels and their relatives to warrant caution in this instance. There are many more much safer fungi one can eat, and avoid becoming a culinary pioneer into little known and risky areas!

Helvella lacunosa Afzeli ex Fries
Fruit-body: 5–10cm (2–4in) high
Spores: pale cream, 15–20 x 9–12µm, smooth
Edibility: suspect, best avoided

A strange and rather sombre fungus. The grey-black saddle-like cap is curled down over the stem, which is grey and twisted, fluted with ribs and pits, and is hollow with chambers inside. It grows in mixed woods along tracks and mossy banks, and is quite common in the autumn. There is some doubt as to its edibility in any quantity, so it is best avoided.

Gyromitra infula (Schaeffer ex Fries) Quélet
Fruit-body: 2.5–10cm (1–4in) high
Spores: cream, 18–23 x 7–8µm, smooth
Edibility: deadly poisonous

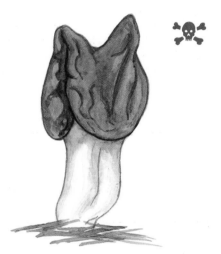

A rare species in Britain, it is found most often in Scotland. It grows on fallen, mossy conifer logs or debris in the autumn. The dark reddish-brown cap is lobed and folded down like a saddle and is curiously wrinkled. The stem is white or flushed pale brown and is smooth on the outside but hollow with some chambers within. This and the following species are notorious for their poisons, which are removed only by thorough cooking. If undercooked, or even if the vapours given off during cooking are inhaled, poisoning can occur. The toxin is now known to be monomethyhydrazine, a constituent of some rocket fuels. It has a cumulative effect and there have been some serious, even fatal poisonings from these species in Europe.

Gyromitra esculenta (Persoon ex Fries) Fries – 'False Morel'
Fruit-body: 5–15cm (2–6in) high
Spores: cream, 18–22 x 9–12µm, smooth
Edibility: deadly poisonous

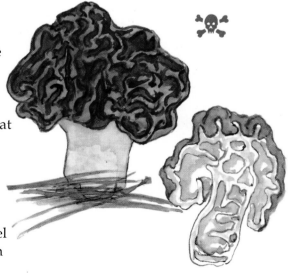

An infamous species and the cause of much misunderstanding; even the specific name *esculenta* is confusing. Although this is widely eaten in Europe and was even purchased in cans in recent years, it has nevertheless caused serious and fatal poisonings. Like the previous species, it contains a cumulative toxin which is destroyed only by the heat of cooking or by boiling off. Unfortunately, the cook often got sick from the fumes while his/her guests were unharmed. It took many years to discover the culprit in this mushroom. The fungus is called False Morel but it looks very little like one. The cap is strangely wrinkled and brain-like with a glossy surface, not pitted and ridged like a Morel. In section the cap and stem are irregularly chambered throughout, whereas a Morel is completely hollow down the middle. This species is rather uncommon but widely distributed under conifers and grows in the spring.

Otidea onotica (Persoon) Fuckel

Fruit-body: 2.5–5cm (1–2in)

Spores: 12–14 x 5–6μm, elliptical, smooth

Edibility: edible but worthless

A lovely species, one of a group sometimes referred to as rabbit's ears because of their shape. The irregular, lobed cup is long and ear-like and a bright peach-yellow to ochre, darker and more orange inside (which is lined with the asci). One or more 'ears' may be fused together at the base to form a clump. It is rather uncommon and grows on soil and leaf litter in mixed woods. The similar *O. leporina* is a much duller ochre.

Peziza vesiculosa Bulliard

Fruit-body: 2.5–7.5cm (1–3in)

Spores: 20–24 x 12–14μm, elliptical, smooth

Edibility: inedible

There are many species of *Peziza*, all popularly referred to as cup fungi. They vary in size and colour but are mostly shades of ochre, brown to grey-violet. This is one of the more distinctive species and often grows in large clusters. The yellow-ochre cup is paler, whitish and very rough and scurfy-granular on the outer surface. The margin of the cup is jagged, tooth-like or blistered. This species likes areas with old straw or compost, or old manure heaps, and is widespread everywhere.

Peziza michelii (Boudier) Dennis

Fruit-body: 2.5–10cm (1–4in)

Spores: 17–21 x 8–10μm, elliptical and finely warted

Edibility: edible but worthless

One of a number of dark brown species, this one has an attractive violet or purple hue on the outer surface. The inner surface of the cup is flushed with olive. It often appears a little earlier in the season and may even appear in the spring. It is found in leaf litter and is widespread but uncommon.

Aleuria aurantia (Fries) Fuckel –
'Orange Peel Fungus'
>   **Fruit-body**: 2.5–10cm (1–4in)
>
>   **Spores**: 18–22 x 9–10µm, elliptical, with a network
>   of fine ridges
>
>   **Edibility**: edible

A beautiful species which really can look like pieces
of orange peel – and vice versa. The bright, clear
orange cups are round to irregular in outline and
much paler on the outside, which is also rather
scurfy-granular. It grows often in large groups and
may appear scattered along track sides or in
disturbed areas, and is quite common in some years.

Scutellinia scutellata (Linnaeus ex Fries)
Lamb
>   **Fruit-body**: 0.6–1cm (¼–½in)
>
>   **Spores**: 18–19 x 10–12µm, elliptical and warted
>
>   **Edibility**: inedible

Although only just making it as a larger fungus, it is
included here because with a hand-lens it is a truly
beautiful species and is easily spotted in the forest if
you look closely at wet, rotted logs. The bright, deep
scarlet cups are quite round and the margin is fringed
with a row of black eyelash-like hairs. The underside
of the cup is minutely hairy. There are a number of
species which are distinguished microscopically, and
the length of the lashes and the size of the cup varies
depending on the species concerned, but they are
otherwise very similar. Common everywhere.

Trichoglossum hirsutum (Persoon)
Boudier – 'Earth Tongue'
>   **Fruit-body**: 2.5–7.5cm (1–3in)
>
>   **Spores**: enormously long and thin, 100–150 x 6–7µm,
>   brown and divided into 16 chambers
>
>   **Edibility**: inedible

Difficult to spot against the forest floor, these black,
velvety clubs or tongues are very common. There
are a number of species, all looking very similar and
needing a microscope to identify them. Their spores
differ in the number of chambers within. The
surface of the club in *Trichoglossum* is minutely
velvety, in contrast to the almost identical
Geoglossum, which is smooth.

Leotia lubrica Persoon ex Fries – 'Jelly Babies'
Fruit-body: 2.5–5cm (1–2in)
Spores: 17–26 x 4–6μm, spindle-shaped
Edibility: inedible

Like the sweets of that name, this fungus does rather resemble jelly babies. There is a rounded, rubbery-jelly cap coloured ochre to slightly greenish, with a rubbery yellow stem which may be roughened and granular with darker dots. It can grow in large clusters and is common in leaf litter everywhere. Other species have deep olive or blackish-green caps.

Chlorociboria aeruginascens (Nylander) Karsten
Fruit-body: 0.6cm (¼in)
Spores: 6–10 x 1.5–2μm, spindle-shaped
Edibility: inedible

One more often finds the effects of this fungus than the fungus itself. If you walk through any woodland, especially where there are oak trees present, and examine any fallen branches, you will almost certainly find some stained a bright bluish-green. This is the wood that was used to make green inlaid furniture called Tunbridge Ware and was highly valued for its unusual colour. The stain is produced by a tiny cup fungus which fruits only rarely. When they are found the cups are flattened, with a tiny stem, and are a vivid and intense blue-green. It is widespread everywhere.

Bulgaria inquinans (Persoon) Fries – 'Rubber Buttons'
Fruit-body: 1-5cm (½–2in)
Spores: 9–17 x 6–7.5μm, the acsi contain eight spores, the upper four brown and kidney-shaped, the lower four colourless but similarly shaped
Edibility: inedible

Unmistakable when mature, these strange, rubbery-textured buttons are quite common everywhere. The outer surface may be brownish and roughened, while the inner surface is black and smooth. It grows on fallen branches and logs of oak and beech and appears in the autumn.

Tuber aestivum Vittadini – 'Summer Truffle'
Fruit-body: 2.5–10cm (1–4in)
Spores: brownish, elliptical, 25–50 x 17–37μm, with a network of ridges
Edibility: One of the best known edibles

Truffles are perhaps the most exotic, and certainly the most expensive of edible mushrooms. In Europe, where most truffles are collected for food, a 'Truffle tree' is usually guarded as if it were a costly work of art and trespassers often face fierce dogs or even gunfire! The species shown here is not the most highly prized – that is *Tuber melanosporum*, which does not occur in England – but is still greatly valued for its pungent, intense odour and flavour. Only a thin sliver is needed to flavour a dish. The lumpy, warted skin is blackish-brown while the interior is whitish-buff with convoluted veins. It grows under ground near mixed deciduous trees and likes lime-rich soils. The traditional method of finding them involves dogs or pigs which are trained to track them by their scent and they are still used today with great effectiveness.

Choiromyces meandriformis Vittadini
Fruit-body: 5–12.5cm (1–5in)
Spores: 18–20μm, covered with blunt warts
Edibility: edible but not highly valued

One of the commoner truffles to be found because, unlike most other species, it often pushes up above the surface of the soil. The lumpy, irregular ball is ochre to pinkish-ochre and often bruises reddish-brown. The interior is whitish, veined and has a strong fruity odour. It is widespread in England and Europe under mixed deciduous trees.

Daldina concentrica (Bolton ex Fries) Cesat & de Notaris G. – 'King Alfred's Cakes'; 'Cramp Balls'
Fruit-body: 2.5–7.5cm (1–3in)
Spores: black, elliptical, bean-shaped, 14-16 x 6-8μm
Edibility: hard, inedible

This strange, cushion-like fungus is hard and woody to touch. The outer surface is dull reddish-brown, turning black when old, while the interior, if cut vertically, reveals concentric rings of black and white. The spore producing asci are grouped in small 'flasks', called perithecia, and these are arranged in a layer under the crust-like surface with tiny apertures opening on to the surface. An interesting feature is that the spores are ejected only during hours of darkness.

Xylaria carpophila (Persoon) Fries
Fruit-body: 2.5–5cm (1–2in) high
Spores: brown, 12–13 x 5–5.5µm, elliptical
Edibility: inedible

Easily distinguished by its very specific habitat of fallen beech husks, the thin woody 'antlers' are often irregular or flattened, sometimes branched, and have a lumpy, tuberculate surface. They are blackish with whitish tips and may often be overlooked since they are easily covered with fallen leaves. A number of stems may emerge from one husk.

Cordyceps capitata (Holmskjold ex Fries) Link
Fruit-body: 5–10cm (2–4in) high
Spores: rode-like,16–21 x 2–3µm
Edibility: Unknown

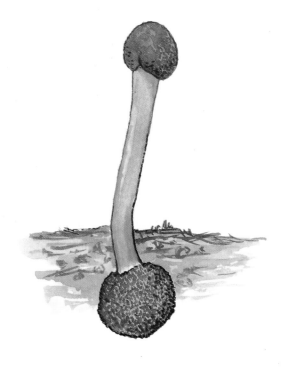

Another fungus that is extremely specific in its growth, this species is found attached to subterranean false truffles of the genus *Elaphomyces*. The rounded, fertile head is a pale orange-brown while the sterile stem is a paler ochre, sharply marked off from the head. The mycelium at the base is whitish (not yellow as in *C. ophioglossoides*, see page 179). It is rather uncommon, and difficult to detect against the forest floor, and prefers moss and needle litter in coniferous woods.

Cordyceps militaris (Linnaeus ex Fries) Link
Fruit-body: 2.5–5cm (1–2in) high
Spores: thread-like, 200 x 2µm, multiply septate
Edibility: inedible

A vividly coloured and remarkable fungus, widespread but not common, this again has a very specific choice of habitat. It is a parasite of the buried pupal stages of various butterflies and the mycelium invades and spreads throughout the insect body. The bright reddish or orange heads are hardly to be confused with anything else and when viewed closely are seen to be densely roughened and punctate. The stems are paler, yellowish and mottled with orange. Many clubs may emerge from one insect pupa.

Xylaria hypoxylon (Linnaeus ex Hook)
Greville – 'Candle-snuff'
> **Fruit-body**: 2.5–8cm (1–3in)
> **Spores**: black, 11–14 x 5–6μm, bean-shaped
> **Edibility**: inedible

Growing on fallen timber and old stumps everywhere, this small fungus looks like the snuffed-out wick of a candle. The tough, black stem may fork several times and is white and powdery at the tip. The white powder is formed of large, asexual spores; later it will turn black as the sexual spores mature.

Xylaria polmorpha (Persoon ex Mérat)
Greville – 'Dead Man's Fingers'
> **Fruit-body**: 5–10cm (2–4in)
> **Spores**: black, 20–30 x 5–10μm, spindle-shaped
> **Edibility**: inedible

The gruesome common name always intrigues, but once you find this fungus you will see that it is quite apposite. It does indeed produce clumps (often more than five) of fat, bloated or misshaped 'fingers', which are black and hard. The surface is dry and roughened or granular. If sectioned, the flesh is white inside. The asci are formed in tiny chambers or flasks set in the tough rind with their apertures pointing outwards. This species may also sometimes be white and powdery from a layer of asexual spores. It grows on buried wood or old stumps and is very common everywhere.

Cordyceps ophioglossoides (Ehrhart ex Fries) Link
> **Fruit-body**: 5–10cm (2–4in)
> **Spores**: enormously long and thin, but breaking apart into 2.5–5 x 2μm, elliptical-cylindrical units, smooth
> **Edibility**: inedible

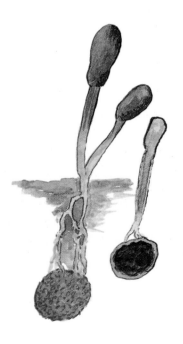

A strange fungus, which is a member of a large group that all specialize in parasitizing some other organism, usually insects. In this instance, however, the host is another fungus. If you carefully trace down the golden mycelial threads which emerge from the base of the stem, you will eventually come to a small, brown ball which is the False Truffle, *Elaphomyces*. Although a common species, it is difficult to spot on the forest floor and it takes great care to unearth the False Truffle.

GLOSSARY

Acrid Producing a burning sensation on the tongue.

Adnate Referring to gills, or lamellae, which join the stem for most of their width.

Ammonia (NH$_3$) A 5% solution (household glass-cleaner with ammonia will often do just as well) is very useful. It causes reactions ranging from bright red to violet or green.

Amyloid A blue-black reaction of fungal tissue or spores to the iodine solution - Melzer's iodine.

Apiculus A point or short stalk at one end of the spore.

Ascus The usually cylindrical cell containing the spores in the Ascomycete fungi.

Basidia Club-like cells on which the spores are produced.

Caespitose Growing in clusters or clumps, with the stems joined at the base.

Capillitium Sterile threads in the spore-mass (gleba) of a Gasteromycete.

Clavate Club-shaped.

Cuticle The outer skin of the cap or stem.

Cystidium Specialized cells on any part of the mushroom, often very distinctive in shape.
Decurrent Referring to gills which run down the stem at the point of attachment.

Deliquescing Gills dissolving into a fluid, liquefying.

Dextrinoid A reddish-brown reaction in cells or spores in response to the iodine solution - Melzer's Iodine.

Ferrous sulphate (FeSO$_4$) A 10% solution is very important in testing many fungi, especially the genus *Russula.* Common reactions are blue, green or pinkish-salmon.

Fibrillose With fine fibres.

Fibrous With coarse fibres.

Filamentous Composed of fine filaments or thread-like cells.

Floccose Woolly, or with small tufts of fibres.

Gleba The compacted mass of spores and spore-producing basidia formed inside the fruiting body of a Gasteromycete fungus.

Globose Roughly spherical.

Hygrophanous Changing colour as the tissues dry out.

Hymenium The fertile layer of cells that produces spores.

Infundibuliform Funnel-shaped.

KOH *See* Potassium Hydroxide.

Lamellae Also called gills, these are the radial flaps of tissue on which the basidia are formed in the Agaricales.

Latex The sticky fluid exuded from the tissues of some mushrooms, especially *Lactarius* and *Mycena.*

Mealy Can refer to a granular appearance *or* to an odour of fresh ground meal.

Melzer's Solution A specialized iodine solution made up of: 0.5gm iodine, 1.5gm potassium iodide, 20ml water, 20ml chloral hydrate. It is an essential reagent for many fungi, for determining the amyloid (blue-black), dextrinoid (reddish-brown), or negative reactions of spores, tissues etc.

Mycelium The mass of fine threads (hyphae) that make up the fungus, and which runs through the soil or other substrate.

Mycorrhiza A beneficial association in which nutrients are exchanged between fungal hyphae and plant roots or tissues.

Network A fine, often minutely raised, mesh-like pattern of thin ridges running over the stem of a mushroom or the surface of spores.

Peridiole The small seed- or egg-like capsule that contains the spores in a Bird's Nest fungus.

Peridium The outer wall of the spore case in many Gasteromycetes.

Peristome The opening at the apex of the spore-sac in an earthstar (*Geastrum*).

Perithecium A flask-shaped chamber of spore-producing asci in some Ascomycetes.

Potassium hydroxide (KOH). Usually found as a 5% solution, this is the standard reagent for testing many mushrooms and for softening dried specimens.

Pruinose Frosted or with a grape-like 'bloom'.

Reticulum A fine network.

Rhizomorph A root- or string-like bundle of tough mycelial hyphae.

Septate Partitioned with one or more cross-walls.

Sinuate Referring to gills that curve up, or are notched where they join the stem.

Squamulose With minute scales.

Striate With fine parallel lines.

Subglobose Not perfectly rounded.

Substrate The surface on which a fungus lives and feeds.

Tomentose Finely velvety.

μm, micrometre or micron $\frac{1}{1000}$ of a millimetre.

Umbilicate With a central depression, or navel, in the cap.

Umbo A central hump, or dome, in the cap.

Vinaceous Wine-red, purplish-red.

Viscid Sticky, glutinous when wet.

Volva Membranous bag, or sac, out of which some mushrooms emerge.

Zonate With cap or flesh concentrically zoned.

TYPICAL MUSHROOM CLASSIFICATION: FLY AGARIC	
Kingdom	Fungi
Division	Eumycota
Subdivision	Basidiomycotina
Class	Basidiomyctes
Subclass	Holobasidiomycetes
Order	Agaricales
Family	Amanitaceae
Genus	*Amanita*
Species	*A. muscaria*

BIBLIOGRAPHY

The following list is divided into general works of interest to most amateurs, and specialist volumes for those who wish to pursue the subject further. These include a number of important monographs and studies of individual genera. A few older, out of print, general books are included that still stand the test of time as good field guides; these should still be available from public libraries. Most mycologists end up with many different field guides and reference works, because each will usually have something unique to offer by way of information or species illustrated.

GENERAL BOOKS:

Mushrooms and other fungi of Great Britain and Europe, Roger Phillips (Pan, 1981).
Still in print, this photographic guide should be on everyone's bookshelf. It covers over 900 species and is the most complete reference work in one volume available. The photographs are superb, and show the mushrooms from many angles. Larger than a field guide, it is nevertheless taken into the woods by many mycologists!

The Mushrooms and Toadstools of Britain and North-western Europe, Marcel Bon (Hodder & Stoughton, 1987).
Another essential field guide for both beginner and enthusiast, this book illustrates over 1200 species, with brief descriptions and spore outlines. The nomenclature is often different from other contemporary guides, although synonyms are usually given.

Collins Guide to Mushrooms and Toadstools, Morten Lange & F. Bayard Hora (Collins, 1978). For many years this was *the* field guide to use.

The colour plates were taken from a much larger, and sadly almost impossible to obtain set of volumes by J. Lange (see the specialist list below) and still stand the test of time today. Most libraries have a copy.

Mushrooms and Toadstools, A Study of the Activities of Fungi, John Ramsbottom (Collins, 1969, recently reprinted as a facsimile volume). Undoubtedly the most fascinating and engrossing book ever written on the natural history of fungi; it covers every aspect of their life, history, folklore, etc. Try to obtain the original volume, which has much better quality printing and colour photographs.

JOURNALS:

The Mycologist (Cambridge University Press for the British Mycological Society).
This quarterly journal is aimed at all levels of interest in mycology, and is illustrated with many good quality colour photographs. It is available by subscription from the publisher. Anyone interested in fungi should read this authoritative and interesting journal and, of course, should apply to join the British Mycological Society, details of which are given in the journal.

SPECIALIST WORKS:

British Fungus Flora Agarics and Boleti, Vols. 1-6, D.M. Henderson, R. Watling, P.D. Orton & N.M. Gregory (Royal Botanic Garden, Edinburgh, 1970-1991). Appearing in parts, this continuing series consists of essential monographs of British species in the Boletaceae, Coprinaceae, Bolbitiaceae, Pluteaceae, Strophariaceae and Pleurotaceae, among others. It includes full keys with line drawings.

British Ascomycetes, R.W.G. Dennis (J.Cramer, 1978).

The standard reference work on the British and Northern European Cup fungi, and allied fungi.

Keys to British Species of Russula, R.W. Rayner (The British Mycological Society, 1985. Address: c/o CAB International, Mycological Institute, Ferry Lane, Key, Richmond, Surrey, TW9 3AF). An extremely thorough and ingenious set of keys to all the British species known up to 1985 (115 species), with line drawings.

Key to the Gasteromycetes of Great Britain, V. Demoulin & J.V.R. Marriott (The British Mycological Society, 1981). The only modern set of keys to this group in English.

Guide to the Literature for the Identification of British Fungi, M. Holden (The British Mycological Society, 1982). An exhaustive list of all important works on British fungi, old and new; the best place to start investigating the literature.

Keys to Agarics and Boleti, M. Moser (Roger Phillips, 1983). This is a translation of the original German work, and is a set of keys to almost every species ever recorded from Northern Europe, an essential work of reference.

Fungi of Switzerland, Vols. 1-3, J. Breitenbach, F. Kränzlin (Verlag Mykologia, 1984-91). A remarkable set of colour photographs covering the Ascomycetes, Gasteromycetes, Aphyllophorales, Boletes, and part of the Agaricales, with further parts in production. Every species also has microscopic characters illustrated. The most up-to-date and thorough work available, it is very expensive, but a major reference work for years to come. Most species occur in Britain.

Flora Agaricina Danica, J.E. Lange (Copenhagen, 1935-40). A very expensive set of five volumes, now no longer in print, but available in many reference libraries. It consists of hundreds of beautiful watercolour paintings and has been a standard reference for many years to the fungi of Northern Europe. Worth tracking down just to admire the artwork and daydream of owning your own set!

FUNGAL CLASSIFICATION

CLASS: BASIDIOMYCETES. Fungi with spores formed externally, on basidia.

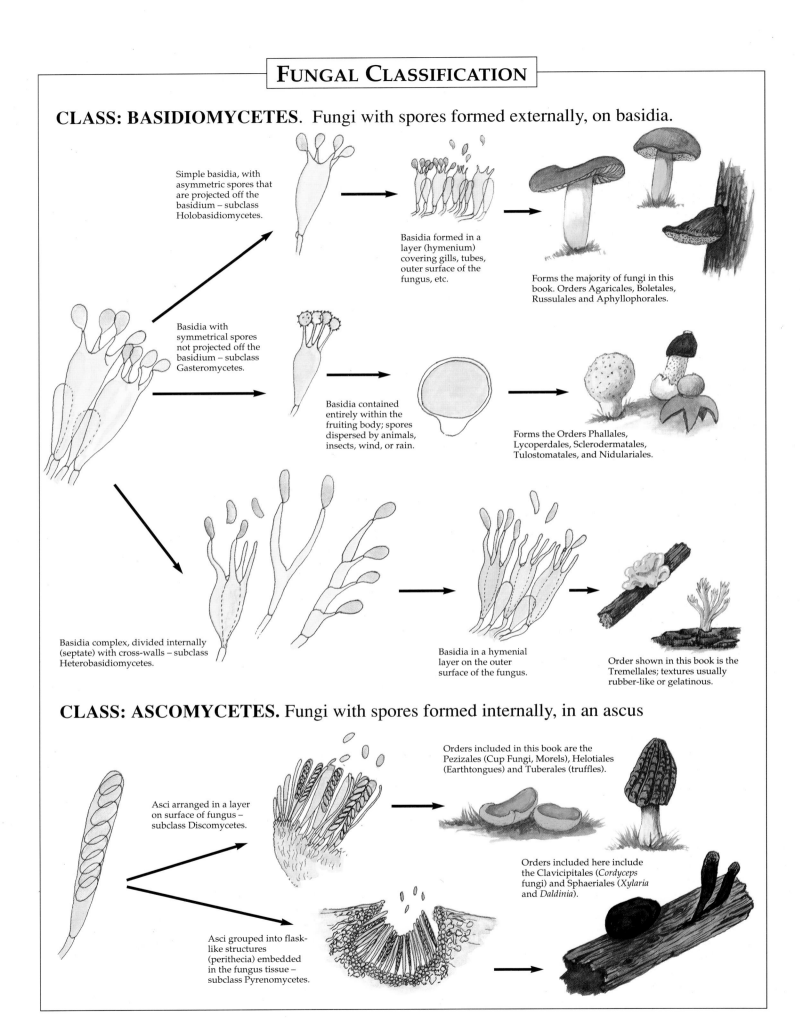

Simple basidia, with asymmetric spores that are projected off the basidium – subclass Holobasidiomycetes.

Basidia formed in a layer (hymenium) covering gills, tubes, outer surface of the fungus, etc.

Forms the majority of fungi in this book. Orders Agaricales, Boletales, Russulales and Aphyllophorales.

Basidia with symmetrical spores not projected off the basidium – subclass Gasteromycetes.

Basidia contained entirely within the fruiting body; spores dispersed by animals, insects, wind, or rain.

Forms the Orders Phallales, Lycoperdales, Sclerodermatales, Tulostomatales, and Nidulariales.

Basidia complex, divided internally (septate) with cross-walls – subclass Heterobasidiomycetes.

Basidia in a hymenial layer on the outer surface of the fungus.

Order shown in this book is the Tremellales; textures usually rubber-like or gelatinous.

CLASS: ASCOMYCETES. Fungi with spores formed internally, in an ascus

Asci arranged in a layer on surface of fungus – subclass Discomycetes.

Orders included in this book are the Pezizales (Cup Fungi, Morels), Helotiales (Earthtongues) and Tuberales (truffles).

Orders included here include the Clavicipitales (*Cordyceps* fungi) and Sphaeriales (*Xylaria* and *Daldinia*).

Asci grouped into flask-like structures (perithecia) embedded in the fungus tissue – subclass Pyrenomycetes.

INDEX

A

abruptibulbus, Agaricus **see** essettei, A.
adspersum, Ganoderma **see** applanatum, G.
aereus, Boletus 19
aeruginascens, Chlorociboria 176
aeruginascens, Suillus 35
aeruginea, Russula 40
aeruginosa, Stropharia 106
aestivalis, Boletus 19
aestivum, Tuber 177
Agaricaceae 100-4
Agaricales 54-134
Agaricus 100-4
Agrocybe 127-8
alba, citrina var., Amanita 86
albidus, Boletus 21
albonigra, Russula 38
alboviolaceus, Cortinarius 117
Aleuria 175
alliaceus, Marasmius 78
alnicola, Pholiota 126
Amanita 83-91
Amanitaceae 83-91
Amanitopsis = Amanita 84-6
amethystea, Laccaria 67
amethystina, Clavulina 142
amianthinum, Cystoderma 76
amoena, Russula 45
amoenolens, Russula 46
androsaceus, Marasmius 77
annulosulphurea, rubescens var., Amanita 89
Aphyllophorales 135-53
appendiculatus, Boletus 21
applanatum, Ganoderma 152
aquifluus, Lactarius = L. helvus 49
areolatum, Scleroderma **see** S. verrucosum
argentatus, Cortinarius 117
Armillaria 62-63
armillatus, Cortinarius 116
Artist's Fungus 152
arvensis, Agaricus 102
Ascomycetes 9, 16, 169-79
Ascus 9
asema , butyracea var., Collybia 79
aspera, Amanita = A. franchetii 90
aspera, Cystolepiota 94
aspera, Lepiota = Cystolepiota aspera 94
Astraeaceae 161
Astraeus 161
atramentarius, Coprinus 111
atropurpurea, Russula 44
atrotomentosus, Paxillus 112
augustus, Agaricus 102
aurantia, Aleuria 175

aurantiaca, Hygrophoropsis 64
aurantiacum, Leccinum 31
aurantiorugosus, Pluteus 134
aurantium, Tricholoma 72
aurea, Ramaria 138
Aureoboletus 27
auricula-judae, Auricularia 166
Auricularia 166
Auriculariaceae 166
Auriscalpium 146
aurivella, Pholiota 125
auroturbinatus, Cortinarius 115

B

badius, Boletus 28
badius, Polyporus **see** varius, P.
Basidiomycetes 9, 17-168
basidium 9
Battareae 163
battareae, Amanita 85
Beefsteak Polypore 153
berkeleyi, Hygrocybe = H. pratensis 54
bernardii, Agaricus 101
bertillonii, Lactarius **see** vellereus, L.
betularum, Russula 41
betulinus, Lenzites **see** quercina, D.
betulinus, Piptoporus 150
bicolor, Laccaria 67
Birch Polypore 150
Bird's Nest Fungi 164-5
birnbaumi, Leucocoprinus 95
bitorquis, Agaricus 101
Bleeding Mycena 81
blennius, Lactarius 53
Blusher 89
bohemica, Lepiota = Macrolepiota rhacodes 97
bolaris, Cortinarius 118
Bolbitiaceae 127-8
Bolbitius 127
Boletaceae 18-36
Boletales 18-36
Boletus 19-28
bombycina,Volvariella 134
bongardii, Inocybe 121
botrytis, Ramaria 139
bovinus, Boletus 35
Bovista 159
bovista, Scleroderma **see** citrinum, S.
Bracket Fungi 147-53
Brick Caps 107
brumale, Tulostoma 163
brumalis, Polyporus 147
brunneoincarnata, Lepiota 93
bryanti, Geastrum **see** pectinatum G.
bucknallii, Cystolepiota 94
bucknallii, Lepiota = Cystolepiota bucknalli 94
bulbosa, Armillaria = A. lutea 63
Bulgaria 176
butyracea, Collybia 79

C

P

Paddy Straw Mushroom 134
pallida, pratensis var., *Hygrocybe* 54
palmatus, Rhodotus 129
paludosa, Agrocybe see praecox, A.
Panaeolina = Panaeolus 108
Panaeolus 108
Panellus 60
Panther Cap 88
pantherina, Amanita 88
Panus 60
parasitica, Asterophora see lycoperdoides, A.
parasiticus, Boletus 27
Parasol Mushroom 96
parazurea, Russula 39
Parrot Mushroom 56
patouillardii, Inocybe 122
Paxillaceae 112
Paxillus 112
pectinatum, Geastrum 160
pelianthina, Mycena 82
penarius, Hygrophorus 58
Pennybun 19
pergamenus, Lactarius see piperatus, L.
perlatum, Lycoperdon 158
petasatus, Pluteus 133
Peziza 174
Phaeocollybia 123
Phallales 154-6
phalloides, Amanita 83
phalloides, Battareae 163
Phallus 154-5
Pholiota 124-6
Phylloporus 112
Phyllotopsis 59
picaceus, Coprinus 110
picta, Xeromphalina see campanella, X.
pilatianus, Agaricus see xanthodermus, A.
pinophilus, Boletus 20
piperatus, Boletus 27
piperatus, Lactarius 51
Piptoporus 150
pisciodora, bongardii var., *Inocybe* 121
Pisolithus 162
pistillaris, Clavariadelphus 140
placomyces, Agaricus 103
platyphylla, Megacollybia 74
platyphylla, Tricholomopsis = Megacollybia 74
Pleurotaceae 59-60
Pleurotus 59
plicatilis, Coprinus 111
plumbea, Bovista 159
Pluteaceae 133-4
Pluteus 133-4
poetarum, Hygrophorus see penarius, H.
Poison Pie 120
polygramma, Mycena 82
polymorpha, Xylaria 179
Polyporaceae 147-53

Polyporus 147-8
porosporus, Boletus 25
Porphyrellus 36
porphyria, Amanita 87
porphyrophaeum, Entoloma 131
porphyrosporus, Porphyrellus 36
portentosum, Tricholoma 71
Postia 150
praecox, Agrocybe 127
pratense, Vascellum 157
pratensis, Hygrocybe 54
Prince Mushroom 102
procera, Lepiota = Macrolepiota procera 96
procera, Macrolepiota 96
proxima, Laccaria 68
pruinatus, Boletus 25
prunulus, Clitopilus 130
Psathyrella 109
pseudoconica, Hygrocybe see conica, H.
Pseudocraterellus 136
pseudosalor, Cortinarius 114
pseudoscaber, Porphyrellus 36
pseudosulphureus, Boletus 22
Psilocybe 106-7
psittacina, Hygrocybe 56
Pterula 140
pubescens, Lactarius see torminosus, L.
pudens, Xerula see radicata, X.
puellaris, Russula 42
Puffballs 157-9
pulmonarius, Pleurotus see ostreatus, P.
pulverulentus, Boletus 28
punicea, Hygrocybe 55
puniceus, Cortinarius = C. sanguineus 119
pura, Mycena 81
purpurascens, Cortinarius 116
purpureum, Chondrostereum 143
pyriforme, Lycoperdon 158
pyrogalus, Lactarius 50
pyrotricha, Psathyrella see velutina, P.
pyxidata, Omphalina 61

Q

queletii, Boletus 23
quercina, Daedalea 151
quercinum, Leccinum 31
quietus, Lactarius 53

R

radicata, Oudemansiella = Xerula radicata 76
radicata, Xerula 76
radicosum, Hebeloma 120
Ramaria 138
Ramariaceae 138-40
Ramariopsis see Clavulinopsis
ramosum, Hericium 145
Red Caps 31
Red Staining Mushroom 103
regius, Boletus 20